"You'll marry ~~me...~~ managed to sound calm, but inside she was a nervous wreck, *praying* he said yes. And somehow dreading that yes at the same time.

"Marry you? I thought you were brilliant, *cara*. Why would I have met you in public, for many to see, if not to plant the romantic seeds of our engagement?"

She could not stop herself from pulling a face at the word *romantic*.

Luciano chuckled. "You will need to work on your acting skills."

"Indeed." She cleared her throat. "But, if you did not notice the papers this morning, I have already planted my own seeds."

She pulled her phone out of her purse, brought up one of the gossip channels that had the picture she'd arranged. Then she slid the phone across the table to him.

He picked it up. "Look at you, Serena," he murmured, studying the picture, then smiled, his gaze sharp and on her. A flutter centered in her chest. Like nerves, but warmer. She didn't understand it.

Or like it.

Lorraine Hall is a part-time hermit and full-time writer. She was born with an old soul and her head in the clouds, which, it turns out, is the perfect combination to spend her days creating thunderous alpha heroes and the fierce, determined heroines who win their hearts. She lives in a potentially haunted house with her soulmate and rambunctious band of hermits-in-training. When she's not writing romance, she's reading it.

Books by Lorraine Hall

Harlequin Presents

The Forbidden Princess He Craves
Playing the Sicilian's Game of Revenge
A Diamond for His Defiant Cinderella

The Diamond Club

Italian's Stolen Wife

Rebel Princesses

His Hidden Royal Heirs
Princess Bride Swap

Work Wives to Billionaires' Wives

The Bride Wore Revenge

Visit the Author Profile page
at Harlequin.com.

A WEDDING BETWEEN ENEMIES

LORRAINE HALL

PRESENTS

Harlequin® PRESENTS™

ISBN-13: 978-1-335-93983-8

A Wedding Between Enemies

Recycling programs for this product may not exist in your area.

Harlequin Enterprises ULC
22 Adelaide St. West, 41st Floor
Toronto, Ontario M5H 4E3, Canada
www.Harlequin.com

Printed in Lithuania

MIX
Paper | Supporting responsible forestry
FSC® C021394

A WEDDING BETWEEN ENEMIES

For all the animal lovers.

CHAPTER ONE

SERENA VALLI KNEW two things with full certainty.

First, and most importantly, she hated Luciano Ascione with the fire of at least four generations of fury behind her.

Second, and quite unfortunately, she needed him.

Luckily, he needed her as well. If he cared at all. Which was certainly up for debate.

They were both failing, drowning, and about to implode if they did not reach out and save each other.

She supposed it was the kind of poetic justice born of their fathers—sworn enemies from birth—dying in the same automobile crash. As if they'd both been racing toward something but, so focused on each other, they hadn't been able to reach that end goal.

Serena was determined to learn this lesson her father hadn't. If it meant proposing a deal with her sworn enemy, she would swallow that sword.

Because neither Serena Valli nor Valli Shipping would give in without a fight, no matter how brutal. How demoralizing. How *embarrassing*. Her feelings didn't matter— only the fate of her legacy did.

If there was any way to honor her father's memory—and more importantly, her grandfather's—it was this.

She'd grieved, she supposed. In her way. In the Valli way. There was, after all, no great affection between father and daughter. There had been respect—hers given out of duty, while she'd had to earn his with perfection, and so she had. Serena believed in duty.

And she would continue to do her duty for the Valli name and business, for her legacy. And with that as her mantra, she stepped into the lion's den.

Luciano had never bothered himself with his father's company, Ascione International—the biggest issue they both faced right there in the company's name. Valli had Italian shipping under lock. Ascione fared better in global waters.

Both were being encroached on by an upstart American company, slithering through the cracks left in Valli since her father's death last year. She knew Ascione also suffered cracks, though she doubted Luciano knew.

It was well known he was a thoughtless, careless, reprobate. The one and only thing he'd *ever* accomplished on his own was this club she ventured into now.

He'd inherited everything else and was likely to run that inheritance into the ground. She could let him, but she was afraid if she did, their new rival would win. But if she could manage this, Ascione and Valli working together, they would take down their *mutual* enemy, instead of each other.

Serena would swoop in. She would save everything. And if there was the opportunity, she would do what her father had never been capable of.

Take Ascione down for good.

But for now, she needed them. Or Luciano anyway.

Serena did not spend her time in *clubs*. The dim lights, the pulsing music, the crowds of bodies appealed to her not at all. The only thing she could say in a positive nature about Luciano's Cattiva Idea was that it did not smell of smoke and alcohol, and the bottom of her shoes did not stick to the floor as she'd expected from reading about places people went to at night to drink and frolic.

Instead, Cattiva Idea was…elegant—too loud, certainly, but with a sophistication underneath all the nonsense of gyrating heirs and heiresses trying to outshine each other.

She *supposed*.

Now she made her way through the tables full of the young and sparkling, wincing only a little at the noise level. She was only twenty-six, young yet, but she felt ancient to all their blatant posturing. Her grandfather had once told her she'd been born an old soul, and she could not deny that she felt like one in the audience of her peers.

She changed her focus from the revelers to the corner of the main floor, where on a raised kind of platform, Luciano sat, his arm draped over the bare shoulders of a beautiful woman Serena thought she recognized from one of her favorite television shows. There was a handful of other people at the table and his section seemed to be roped off. *A VIP section*, she supposed and rolled her eyes.

There was no doubt Luciano was a wealthy man. He was dressed in the best of the best, even if he left a few buttons of his shirt undone, as if the glimpse of olive skin was some kind of temptation, some kind of power move.

Serena did not allow herself delusion. He was a handsome man. All jet-black hair and dark eyes. High cheekbones and a Grecian nose. Full mouth, chiseled jaw. Then there was the height, the broad shoulders. There could be no argument. He was stunningly, classically attractive.

He knew it. He used it. She could disdain him for it, but she could not blame him for it.

She too used whatever tools were at her disposal. It was why she'd donned four-inch heels this evening—so she could be closer in height to him. It was why she hadn't worn a *business* suit, though as she didn't lend herself to the frivolous, her dress *was* black. And probably a little more suited for a work cocktail hour than a youthful club. But she'd uncharacteristically left her hair down, allowed it to curl in all the ways it would instead of taming it into a braid or twist as she preferred. She'd worn makeup more in keeping with a night out than a corporate meeting, and added a few pieces of jewelry, on loan from her mother, a far more ostentatious creature than Serena herself.

Serena took after her father, as her mother so often liked to tell her. A deadly dull vulture in the presence of far more interesting peacocks. It was why after the divorce, Serena had spent more time in her father's home than her mother's.

But deadly dull vultures were *successful*, her father had always liked to say. All peacocks did was strut about.

Luciano was most assuredly a peacock. All feathers and color and no substance. *How* was she going to get through to him when all of her motivations would fall on deaf ears?

You'll figure it out, she told herself sternly.

As she got closer, his dark gaze drifted over to her and sharpened in recognition. She didn't stop walking, but she braced herself for the fight ahead. She held his gaze and walked straight to him. She didn't even look at one of the men she supposed acted as some kind of security for him when the suited hulk held out an arm to stop her.

She held Luciano's gaze. "He'll see me," she said.

And Luciano must have waved his little bodyguard off, because the arm dropped, then the rope, and Serena was allowed to move forward.

Once she got close enough to hear him over the pumping music, he smiled. Like a shark. "Ah, if it isn't Satan herself."

Serena smiled in return. Like a wolf. Because a wolf could swim, but a shark couldn't do a damn thing on land. "Do you really suppose the devil would be a woman, when we all know men are the crux of all our problems? Two men in particular."

This got a laugh out of Luciano's companion.

"*Two* men," he scoffed. His gaze dropped to his glass. "The investigators thought differently."

"*Your* investigators thought differently. The ones not on your payroll blamed both men for foolish, unreasonable speeds. A fact that, knowing our fathers, is undeniable."

"Did you know your father?" he asked, tilting his head, as if to consider such a thing. "It is rather difficult to know a snake."

"Perhaps just as difficult as it might be to know an Ascione scorpion."

"As much as I love our little *tête-à-têtes*, I am busy." He gestured to the woman under his arm.

"I think we both know you are not." She gestured to the club around them. "Per usual. But we do have a problem, and I'd like to discuss a solution with you." She offered a polite smile to the actress who was watching them curiously. "In private."

"I shall pass."

"Do you think I came all this way with something that can simply be *passed* on, Luciano? I know you do not understand how anything important works, what kind of threat there is against your legacy, but I would think you would understand just how dire everything is if I would deign to come to you. In *this* place."

"What's wrong with your legacy?" the actress asked him, innocently enough.

Serena had to bite back a smile when he muttered irritably but stood. "We will discuss this in my office," he said.

She glanced back at the actress, wondering if the woman had purposefully helped her along. A wink told her yes.

Serena chose to take this as a good sign for what was to come. She'd take any good sign in this nightmare.

Luciano marched ahead, and she followed him easily enough. Through throngs of people, into an elevator that a card opened. She assumed only his staff had access to the second floor. After a brief elevator ride, he moved into a hallway, and then into a well-appointed office.

He flipped on the lights, closed the door behind her when she entered, then faced off with her, arms across his chest.

"I do not care for accusations about my *legacy* in front of my companions for the evening."

Serena nodded. "I do apologize," she said, without any sincerity. "Are you unaware then? Perhaps this may come as a surprise to you, perhaps the men actually running Ascione have not filled you in. Or perhaps you simply do not understand—"

"I understand just what Ascione is up against," he all but growled, looking fierce and dangerous.

She would not feel intimidated by that. She had been facing down wealthy, ego-driven men since she'd been a teenager. And she had learned how to come out on top. She had won over her father, which had been no small feat. It had required absolute perfection in everything she did.

And she had achieved that perfection. Still did, even with him gone. She used it as ballast and assurance that she could win over *anyone*.

"Then you know that if you do not do *something* in the next six months, Ascione will have to declare bankruptcy."

His expression shuttered. "I know nothing of the sort."

"Well, *I* do. Valli has more time, because I have been at the reins." She would not admit that her father left her a mess *almost* as big as the one Luciano's had left him. She would not admit that for a very brief period of time, she had been struck by the injustice of him being an imperfect mess while requiring perfection from her. "But there is a simple solution to our problems. A cure for both of us. Like with any cure, it is distasteful and might just kill us both first. Such is the nature of a last resort."

"I am all aflutter, Serena. Do tell me your brilliant plan."

Brilliant? She wished. She was down to desperate.

So, she didn't pretty it up. She didn't start with a lot of excuses or foolish words she didn't mean. She went straight for it.

"Marry me."

Luciano Ascione did not believe in hate. It was a wasted emotion. One that had eaten his father alive. Though he would never admit it to the woman standing before him, it had killed the great Gianluca Ascione just as much as the head on collision with a mountain had.

Luciano had always allowed himself one exception when it came to his relationship with hate. The dastardly Vallis. Most specifically the icy, perfect and damnable Serena Valli.

He hated her and enjoyed that hate almost as much as he enjoyed a salacious woman and an expensive whiskey.

It was a shame Serena was beautiful—that she wielded herself in a way he could not help but respect, if he was a fair man.

Luckily, he was not.

Marry me, she had said.

Chin raised, hazel eyes a sparkling challenge. Shoulders back, wearing the highest of heels that *almost* put her on equal footing with him.

Almost.

What he was really having a hard time getting over was the state of her hair. He wasn't sure he'd ever seen it…like this. A halo of dark curls around her face, untamed and… He'd be tempted to call it wild if he thought Serena Valli was capable of wild.

She was not. She was a cold, calculated *verme*. Like her father before her. But worse, she seemed to have no vices. She did not gamble, as her father had. She did not seem to ever drink to excess, as his had. There were no trails of men, gossip or scandal. She was a robot.

And she was suggesting they *marry*. He knew it was a trick, but he couldn't begin to reason out what the trick might be.

"Perhaps I've had a stroke," he offered, to buy himself some time. Because Luciano did not ever find himself *shocked* or at a loss. Except on the news of his father's demise.

And Serena Valli's marriage proposal.

"You have not. Nor have I, though I can understand the confusion. Instead, it is an extreme solution to an extreme problem. I do not relish it, but do you know the kind of attention we can garner if we marry? Do you know the kind of money we could save if we merged our companies? The absolute stone wall to keep this upstart American out of *our* customers' accounts? I don't expect you to, of course, but I have the spreadsheets for whoever handles actually understanding your legacy for you. I shall e-mail them and answer any questions, if you'd give me the appropriate contact information."

"There's just one little problem," Luciano said, smiling at her. Or perhaps he was only *trying* to smile. Her perfume was poisoning his office with a subtle, romantic floral scent that did not suit the woman at all. Perhaps that left him scowling.

"I hate you?" she supplied brightly.

"Not as much as I hate you."

"This, we can debate later," she said, waving it off like an annoying fly, not the center of both their beings. "This marriage, this merger, has nothing to do with emotions, and everything to do with saving our companies."

"Why should you care about saving Ascione? You don't. So, you are thinking only of saving yourself."

"Yes. Lucky for you, the only way I can save myself is to save you as well. I do not expect your thanks, though will gallantly accept it should you ever be wise enough to extend it."

Thanks. She was always such an incredibly arrogant harridan.

"The attention certainly wouldn't hurt your little club either," she continued, as if he had already agreed. As if he *needed* to agree.

"My club needs no extra attention."

"What billionaire *needs* more, Luciano? They simply take it as their due. Or so I thought."

He hated that he agreed with her. Hated that she was right about Ascione—any of his own money that he infused now would simply draw out the inevitable. He needed more of a plan than just plugging holes with money.

She claimed to have one, but…he did not for the life of him understand what she was attempting to do.

"If you give me the contact information of whoever handles Ascione business for you, I will e-mail them my spreadsheets immediately. I am prepared to give you forty-eight hours to consider my proposal once your staff have explained the situation to you."

It was all so condescending. *She* was condescending. As if he needed *staff* to explain his own legacy to him.

But that was the image he had created. While his father had been alive, Luciano had lived and embodied that role when it came to Ascione—having nothing to do with the company, making sure he lived down to every one of his father's low expectations, while quietly and privately focusing his talents on his club.

But after the accident, Luciano had been forced to catch up. Though he did not allow anyone to know just how much work he'd done there, how much he knew and understood. He'd invented a character, instead, and this was the contact information he gave Serena now.

Alan Emidio was Luciano's "man of business". He answered e-mails, took phone calls, studied P&L statements and all the deadly dull business things Luciano's father had long ago given up on Luciano understanding.

Alan did not attend meetings, take phone calls or interact with anyone but Luciano because he did not exist.

Because Luciano understood just fine, now that he did not have to contend with the weight of his father's impossible moving standards.

"I will expect to hear from you soon," Serena said, with a politeness only *she* wielded like an accusation and a weapon. As if every time she chose the high road, she was sneering at whatever lower road she considered him on.

It was infuriating. "I would not wait up, Serena," he returned, smiling at her with as much charm as he could manage. Because it annoyed her. "I have many…companions lined up for my evening."

He saw the annoyance he'd wanted and an added dose of disgust chase over her face, even as she smiled in return, offered a nod and then turned and left his office.

Marry me, she had said.

Not a question. Not a beg. Not a *joke*. A statement of fact, as if that was the only possible answer to this problem they found themselves in.

Except they were not a *they*. They were enemies. Generations of Ascione and Vallis had fought to take over the shipping world in Genoa. And generation after generation, they had been more obsessed with hurting each other than changing with the times and building a sustainable business that would last.

Luciano had always considered that a waste, and pointless to try to talk his father out of. So he'd found something better to do with his time. He had convinced himself he did not care about his father, or Ascione or legacies.

It was funny what death could do to the things you convinced yourself of.

Still scowling at the door, he moved around his desk and then sat down at his computer. He booted up the profile for Alan Emidio.

She had, of course, already e-mailed him. So Luciano read the missive—businesslike, polite and to the point. There were a handful of attachments, and Luciano ignored everything—his guards, the club manager, his phone buzzing in his pocket—until he'd gone through every last one.

Then he sat back in his chair and cursed, scowling at the screen. She should not have known so much about Ascione. She must have implemented some spy—or more likely, her father had before he'd died.

When his father had been alive, Luciano had not been involved in the business. He had not been deemed worthy. He would not *fight* his father's low opinion of him.

But with the man gone, Luciano had not been able to let Ascione crumble into the sea. He had thought he would, but something ate at him. A surprising need to show a dead man he'd been dead wrong.

He'd been bailing water out of a sinking boat without a lifeline. And still he had not given up, even though Serena was right. Six months, unless he did something drastic, was the most he could eke out of Ascione before failing.

He didn't *need* Ascione, but he wanted it. Alive and whole. Perhaps one last *I told you so* to his father.

He could hardly marry Serena Valli, *merge* their companies. It was ludicrous on many a level. It was beyond drastic. It was insanity.

He could ignore it, but she had information and insights she shouldn't.

And that could not stand.

CHAPTER TWO

SERENA HAD DRIVEN HERSELF, as she liked to do when she wanted to feel most in charge, and she took the long, scenic way home, enjoying the play of light and dark as she drove from Genoa up to her estate.

Serena loved her home. Her privacy. The one place she could go and not worry about being Serena Valli. Even before her father had died, the old Valli castle atop a hill looking out over the Ligurian Sea had been her safe place. Her hideaway and sanctuary.

She had moved there permanently in her early twenties to aid in caring for her ailing grandfather. He'd been ninety-one to her twenty-one, and still she thought he was the one person in the world who'd understood her, and vice versa.

When he'd died two years ago, she'd decided to stay. If there was no one left on earth who understood her, at least this place did.

She drove up the winding pathway to the castle now. It was dark up here—very little artificial light at night. Her headlights led the way, and she could see only the shadow of the old house on the jagged peak of hill.

Her mother called it a morgue. Her father had called it a crumbling atrocity.

Serena had begun to call it *home* and meant it. Because neither her father's ostentatious estate in the city, nor her mother's unending array of apartments, houses, villas—all usually funded by the next man down the line—had ever been home.

She parked in the garage, then moved inside, unlocking and then re-engaging the security system. As was so often her habit, she went straight to her room and began the process of taking Serena Valli off.

The heels went first, then the expensive dress and jewelry, making sure to put her mother's belongings in a little case to be returned as soon as possible. She scrubbed her face clean of makeup, took out her contacts and replaced them with her glasses. Neatly, she put everything back where it belonged.

The house could get drafty at night, so she grabbed a shawl before she went down to her sitting room, where a hot mug of tea, a book and her cats would be waiting for her while a fire crackled cozily in the hearth.

She'd need a good hour to decompress before she could even begin to consider sleep. Leopold immediately meowed at her as she entered the luxurious room she'd done little to change since her grandfather's death.

She knew to anyone else it would appear fussy and outdated. *Elderly* even with its dark woods, floral wallpapers and heaps of shawls and throws, but she loved it, and now that some of the sharp grief of losing her grandfather had softened into a subtle missing him, the room comforted her as her grandfather once had with just his presence.

What she had done was add another kitten—this one after her father's death. She was also considering a bird, though Pierro, her house manager, had threatened to quit over that. Her trio of dogs had been trained as guard dogs and they had their own little outbuilding for the evenings, but she was considering getting a puppy that was *just* a dog. *Just* a companion. To be allowed inside to cuddle up in bed with her and the cats. Something tiny and yappy and wonderful.

Serena loved animals. They were so simple. They could be so loving, and interesting with their own little person-alities. They could be pleased easily with daily meals and attention.

She settled into her chair now and took a sip of tea as Leopold hopped onto her lap, and Kate watched with jeal-ous eyes but did not move from her perch at the window. On a sigh of pleasure, Serena smoothed her hand down Leo-pold's spine, closed her eyes and finally relaxed.

In the quiet, only the sound of the fire crackling, she sipped her tea, but she did not pick up her book. She was exhausted, but she would not be able to sleep.

The solution she had suggested to her sworn enemy was not one she relished, not one she *wanted*. It was simply the only one available to her. And now she'd have to wait—for days, no doubt—to see if Luciano would be smart enough to take such an unfortunate deal.

She worried there. It had always been clear he had no real loyalty to Ascione. She had been surprised, in fact, that he hadn't sold it upon his father's death. It was well known in their world that he would not take over any role in his father's company.

But apparently he'd inherited it all the same.

Now she just had to wait.

"I am good at waiting," she told Leopold as he hopped off her lap, no doubt to go harass Kate.

She let her eyes drift closed for a minute. Maybe if she fell asleep here, she would actually sleep for more than an hour or two, before another worry woke her up.

Then she heard someone enter. Reluctantly, she opened her eyes to see Pierro standing in the doorway. He looked... perplexed, which was unlike him.

"Ms. Valli. I apologize for interrupting, but you have a rather...insistent visitor."

"I am not seeing any visitors at this hour, Pierro. You of all people should be able to see to that." She was in her *pajamas*, with a shawl wrapped around her. Honestly, what would possess Pierro...?

She heard it then. A familiar dark, ill-boding voice some-where in the house. Getting closer by the moment.

"We could call the *polizia*," Pierro offered.

But he knew, as well as she did, that this would be a tactical error and bring all the wrong kind of attention to a problem they were trying to hide. That was why he posed it as a question, rather than going ahead and doing it.

Serena sighed, tried to find some inner center of strength here as she got to her feet.

She'd taken off all of her armor, but she could *hear* him.

"Please, show him in," Serena said between clenched teeth, hoping Pierro could take *some* control of the situation.

"You must be on your best behavior, Leopold," she mur-mured to her younger cat, who had a habit of getting a little rambunctious at night. Sweet Kate was placid in her old age and blinked from her perch in the window.

When Luciano strode into her cozy living room, she was not dressed to be Serena Valli, but she would not let that deter her. She stood, chin up, hazel eyes defiant. The fire that crackled in the hearth and the shawl around her shoulders might give the aura of cozy, but she would not.

He swept in, dressed as he had been in the club. Though his hair looked a little mussed, like he'd raked his fingers through it not all that long ago.

Or, more likely, someone else had.

He stopped on a half-stride, something in his expression moving toward surprise before he managed to hide it away. "You need better security," he said by way of greeting.

"You need to take no for an answer." She clutched the shawl a little tighter at her throat, pretending as though she was dressed in her boardroom best. "What on earth are you doing here at this time of night?"

His gaze perused her then. Took in the thick socks, the pajamas, the glasses, the shawl. His mouth curved ever so slightly in pure amusement, but only for a moment.

He scowled. "Explain to me how you have this information."

"What information?"

"The numbers about my company. The projections. You should not have this information, and I want to know what dastardly things you've done to obtain it."

She was shocked someone had already distilled the information for him. She figured he'd wait forty-eight hours out of spite at the very least. "Surely you did not wake up some poor employee to explain it to you when it could have waited until morning."

"No one should have this information," he said, ignoring her.

She supposed she should have seen this accusation coming. Not *everyone* was as thorough and good with numbers as she was. Certainly, Luciano wasn't. But she'd assumed his man of business would explain *this* to him—how easy it was to know your job if you tried.

"It was easy enough to use what I know of the industry, what public information there is, and then extrapolate accordingly." She shrugged. "I am brilliant, Luciano. Trust me, my father would not have allowed me near his company if I was not. If my choices, my decisions, my outcomes weren't perfect. He had rather outmoded ideas about women in the workplace."

"Perhaps we should have switched fathers, then. Mine often lamented that if I was a woman, at least I'd be good for *something.*"

For a moment, the silence around them was awkward instead of hostile. This sort of admission that they might have been better off in each other's shoes.

Then his scowl intensified, and he stepped forward. "There is no way you simply *surmised* this information."

She supposed his proximity was meant to be intimidating, so she refused to be intimidated. Even as her heart rattled around her chest in an unfamiliar rhythm. Without her heels, she had to look up at him, and she did so now, letting none of her nerves show. She clutched her shawl tight and refused to let herself sound winded by the strange sensations twisting through her. "There is, because I did."

"You will tell me the truth."

"I *am* telling you the truth."

"Do you think I will go along with this ridiculous plan because of some pathetic lie? You will tell me how you got this information, or I will destroy you."

She rolled her eyes, lifted an arm. "Destroy away, Luciano." Because she was already almost there.

Luciano realized he was not handling this well, but that only spurred him on.

She had *rolled her eyes* at him. When he was actually being serious instead of his usual insouciance.

Something brushed up against his legs and he only just stopped himself from jumping back. It looked like a stuffed little ball of fur, but it moved, and then looked up, its cat eyes blinking at him.

"*Che cazzo*, is that *real*?"

The ball of fluff offered a pitiful *meow*. Luciano stared down at it for a full minute until his mind could accept it was another cat to go along with the one perched in the window.

Who *was* this woman sitting in a room better suited to an octogenarian cat lady? He knew she was stuffy, stiff, *annoying*, but he'd still assumed she'd live in something sleek and modern and befitting the CEO of a generationally successful shipping company.

He had not expected her to wear *glasses*. To look somehow…innocent and vulnerable standing there in her pajamas, even as she scowled at him, ever the picture of control.

"I think it would be best if you leave, Mr. Ascione," she said primly, no doubt using the *mister* to remind him of his father. "Your assistant may call mine and set up a meeting whenever you would like to discuss my proposal, at an appropriate time and place, but I will not tolerate accusations against me in my own home, at this hour. Call Mr. Emidio and have him explain to you just how I would have gotten my information *without* whatever nonsense corporate espionage you are accusing me of."

"I do not need to call Mr. Emidio," he ground out.

"Surely he is smart enough to see that anyone with a deep understanding of the industry, and your father's shortcomings, would know how to extrapolate that information. Call Mr.—"

"*I* am Mr. Emidio," he exploded.

Regret was a sharp pain, but he'd never allowed himself to let regret sink its teeth in. When he made a mistake, he embraced it, rolled with it, then made it a success.

Serena stopped short, studied him. "I beg your pardon."

He would not explain to her. He would not compound one mistake with another. She was right. They needed a meeting. A business meeting.

"My assistant will be in touch," he ground out, then turned on a heel and let himself out of the sprawling, *ancient* building. Into the dark, with a shining moon and dazzling stars and the sounds of the sea all around him.

He paused there in the drive, having driven himself over. He took a deep breath, then turned around and stared at the looming shadows of the old castle. A ridiculous place to live. Up here alone with the wind whipping and the sound of waves lapping all around him. There were a few lights on in different windows.

In one, he saw the clear shadowed outline of a cat.

Who the hell was Serena Valli?

Well, he intended to find out.

CHAPTER THREE

SERENA STUDIED THE grainy picture in the video. She listened to the local gossip content creator make wild suppositions about what had happened between two rivals last night at Cattiva Idea. Serena appreciated that the photographer had made sure to circulate a picture from an angle that hid the fact Luciano had his arm around another woman, just as Serena had paid her to do.

If Serena managed to get Luciano to agree to this plan, she had no expectations he'd be faithful to a fake marriage. But she wanted it to look—for the first year at least—as if there *had* been something of a fairy-tale element, a *romance* to their union. Something to get people talking about Valli and Ascione. To get their name out there and interest in both the companies up.

At least while she sorted out all their business problems.

I am Mr. Emidio...

Could he really be that ridiculous to pose as his own man of affairs? Could he actually be that...devious? Yes, of course. Could he be that knowledgeable of Ascione? This she had a harder time believing.

She drummed her fingers against her desk, looking back at the picture that made it look as though Luciano Ascione was giving her a great deal of attention in his very own club. Only she could tell that the smile he'd angled her way was full of venom.

She supposed they all played their roles. Maybe he'd been playing the role of flaky playboy while being anything but.

Except he was most definitely a playboy. There was no faking the array of models, actresses, influencers and the like that he always had on his arm.

This was her biggest battle, besides Luciano agreeing to marry her. While, with enough work, she could look elegant enough, whatever beauty she could create was not over the top. She was all-around average. She could not compete with his usual fare.

She had considered the shared grief angle. It had some positives, and it was believable. Grief made people do all sorts of things. But…and Serena knew this was pride over sense talking, she did not want to spend the next few years pretending losing her father was some great loss. She wasn't sure Luciano *could* pretend that losing his was.

So she had to play up the star-crossed lovers angle. Make everyone believe that for years they had been kept apart by their evil fathers. That their union was preceded by years of denial. Not sudden and out of the blue.

"Ms. Valli?"

Serena looked up from her phone to where her assistant stood in the doorway. She beckoned her inside. "Andrea. Is Mr. Ascione here?"

"I'm afraid not. He's…changed plans."

Serena didn't sneer or growl like she wanted to. She

waited patiently for Andrea to continue, a placid smile on her face.

While inside, she pictured herself putting her hands around Luciano Ascione's neck and squeezing as hard as she could.

"He has sent a car. It will take you to Le Marin, where Mr. Ascione is waiting for your appointment."

Underneath her desk, Serena balled her hands into fists, letting her nails dig into her palms. She kept her voice pleasant. "How kind of him to think of having a meal together. You may tell his driver I will be down momentarily."

Andrea looked at her speculatively but nodded and disappeared. Serena jerked out of her chair and allowed herself approximately one minute of pacing and muttering curses before she went to her office bathroom, touched up her makeup and did her deep breathing exercises.

She hated a change of venue, hated petty games of control, but if she wanted her staff to believe in this marriage as much as she wanted the public to, the acting had to start now. She had to move forward with every step, believing that she would get him to agree with her plan.

And *she* would be in control.

She tried to come up with a simple excuse for driving herself, but in the end it just seemed the easiest and less suspicious thing to take the ride offered by Luciano.

She told Andrea that her meeting with Luciano was most important and that she was not to be interrupted, then left her father's—no, *her*—office building and slid into the car waiting for her.

The drive would not take long, so Serena did not get out

her phone or try to do business. She closed her eyes and went over her mantra.

I am strong. I am sure. I am in charge.

The car pulled to a stop at a private entrance in the back of Le Marin, where a staff member, if the crisp black suit was anything to go by, waited.

Even with this backdoor entrance, people would see her. See them. She did not care for the fact they would have an audience of businesspeople and socialites. People who knew them or of them. People who would *talk*. She did not trust that this was a move made in her best interest.

Or maybe those were the excuses she made for herself so she didn't have to admit she was just mad he'd changed the venue on her, because she'd had a battle plan drawn for a meeting on *her* turf, in *her* office.

And now, she had to adjust.

"You will sway it your own way if need be," she reminded herself. Just as she'd done with the club. She was good on her feet when the situation demanded it.

Now it did.

She got out of the car, was greeted by the staff member, then led through a small, narrow hallway and into a room with a beautiful view of the marina. Not everyone's version of beauty, she knew, but symbolic. Because Ascione and Valli boats, shipping containers and the like were all out there.

And in front of the window was Luciano himself. Dressed on the side of *casual* that normally she would have criticized, but he somehow made it look sophisticated and regal, even without a suit jacket or tie.

He made a striking picture there, with such a background, and his own undeniable beauty. What a shame he should be such a cad.

He stood as she approached. She held out her hand as she would in any business meeting. "Mr. Ascione."

"Serena," he greeted, taking her hand, and then instead of shaking it, turning it to be brought to his mouth. He brushed a kiss over her knuckles, his gaze meeting hers as he did so.

The use of her name, and his mouth, was unwelcome. That was all the strange pressure in her chest was. Irritation and frustration with the situation. Even if that had never made her feel breathless and overwarm, like her heart had decided to run a marathon there in her chest.

"I have gotten us a private table, so we may talk without worry of being overheard," he said, gesturing at it now as he dropped her hand. "Please. Sit."

Serena did not allow herself to move stiffly to the table, even though that is what she felt. She did not allow herself to wipe her hand on her skirt, even though it felt as though that would be the only way to rid the strange warmth from her palm.

She all but had to pry her other hand off her purse once seated, but she did not allow him to read anything uncomfortable in her demeanor.

He might have chosen the venue, but she would remain relaxed and in control. At least on the outside.

A waiter appeared, presenting a bottle of wine. When Luciano approved, he began to pour.

Serena put her hand in front of her glass. "None for me. I will stick with water. Thank you."

"Leave the bottle," Luciano told the waiter, who nodded,

then melted away. "Come, *cara*. We might be celebrating by the end of this conversation."

She smiled sweetly at him but spoke between her teeth. "And we might end up tossing the wine at each other."

His mouth quirked at one side, and something in her chest seemed to mimic the movement. A quick, upturned flutter.

"I would almost like to see it, Serena," he said, his gaze moving over her face. "The ice princess losing her temper."

She held his gaze, but something was tying itself in knots in her stomach. Because losing her temper was never an issue, never much of a challenge. She was excellent at control, but the man across from her was the only man who ever tested that.

She hated that it was *him*, but what could be done? She could not control her insides, but she could control her outsides. Even when it was hard. To lose sight of her control *now* would destroy everything.

She refused to be destroyed. By a foolish car accident or a supposedly charming rival. "I hope you shall hold your breath," she offered. Because sparring with him was not a loss of control, it was a gaining of it. It was a duel. A business negotiation. The careful, planned steps of a fencing match.

Luciano sipped his wine, unbothered, leaning back in his chair so that he was perfectly framed by the beautiful lake outside the windows. If someone had taken his picture, it could have been an advertisement for any number of things, and women would sigh over that lazy smile.

She *hated* that her traitorous insides wanted to do just that. Because if she allowed herself to divorce his personality from the external look of him, she would have some *serious* problems with focus.

Luckily, she knew exactly who he was.

A waiter reappeared with the *primi*. He set a dish down in front of both of them, then disappeared again. Luciano made a big production out of discussing the weather, and Serena was well versed in stalling business tactics, so she played along.

Mainly because she didn't think he expected her to.

When the *secondi* was served, he moved the conversation along to her home. She tried not to stiffen, but it was impossible. She did not want his take on the place that meant so much to her. On the place he never should have been. Part of how she'd gotten by was to develop that inner world, that sanctuary, and keep everyone else out. So that it was safe there.

He'd invaded her safety. Gotten a peek under the curtain, so to speak. She had spent the day telling herself it didn't *really* matter. So he knew she wore glasses and had cats? Maybe it gave him glimpses into private things, but it didn't *change* anything.

But she could tell he understood that it bothered her far more than she wanted it to.

Still, to show her discomfort was to lose, so she sipped her water carefully as he spoke.

"So…unique," he said, almost thoughtfully. "And your sitting room. Quite colorful, when you are, if you'll forgive me for saying so, rarely that."

"I do not wish to be colorful," Serena replied, trying to keep the bite out of her tone. "This does not mean I do not enjoy color."

He made a considering noise. She had no doubt he would draw this out. Make her wait for his answer. So she enjoyed her food. A delicious *tortelli* and *ratatuia*. She had never had a dessert quite like the one served next, so she savored it, only half listening to Luciano prattle on about his club.

If it was to be like this, she could handle a potential marriage. She could pretend to listen to him chattering on while she enjoyed a meal. She could be photographed on occasion with his hand in hers. All of this, she was sure she could handle.

But him being in her space last night had introduced a new doubt, and Serena *hated* doubts. She hated to address them. But the way it had felt to have him in her space, seeing who she was underneath her mask. Having to deal with the unique physical reaction she had to him—one she did not want to parse, but might have to. Because a fake marriage would require, at least on occasion, living together.

Maybe once they'd gotten some of the old clients back, once there were enough stories about them to have *everyone* taking a meeting with Valli, they could move to a marriage that didn't need to look…*real*.

But she had to get there first. Which required this dinner, his agreement and a merger of lives and businesses. It required managing the strange sensations he brought out in her, that tangled with the more familiar and perhaps more welcome irritation.

Valli-Ascione, she reminded herself, unable to stop a frown. The merger was the best thing, she knew, but she hadn't fully swallowed how much credit she was going to have to give the man across from her.

After all the work she'd done, after all the perfection

she'd achieved—first to gain her father's trust, then to clean up the mess he'd left her—and for the rest of their lives, no doubt, Luciano would get more credit for saving their companies than she would. Because this was still a man's world, no matter how much better she was at it.

She reminded herself she didn't *need* credit. Never had. As long as *she* knew she was the mastermind behind this. As long as *she* knew she'd saved Valli, like her father couldn't. As long as she was perfection to all her father's imperfection. *That* was what mattered.

When the waiter put a *caffe* in front of her, she smiled up at him in thanks. How many more minutes would this go on? Usually, her patience was endless, but the mere existence of Luciano reminded her that there were variables in this whole plan that she would not be able to control.

Mainly him.

She flicked a glance at Luciano who was watching her with surprisingly shrewd dark eyes, like he could see through her. When no one did.

Her chest felt oddly tight. The idea of being seen settled in her in tangled ways. Because she did not want *him* to see her, but she missed the easy understanding her grandfather had once given her. So it was both uncomfortable and wistful.

She was glad when he leaned carefully forward, made no attempt to hide the shrewdness in his gaze. He did not signal a change in conversation in any other way. But she knew they would now discuss what she'd actually come here for.

"I am still not wholly convinced that you came to this information on your own," he said, more idly than accusatory.

She sighed, but before she could say anything, he held up a hand.

"However, whether you have a spy, or are as brilliant as you claim, the result is the same. Our companies are failing."

"Thanks to our fathers."

"Indeed. And I have no long-lost love for mine, may he rot in hell along with the rest of the Asciones, but I will not let his failure stain *my* reputation."

She was surprised at the fervent note in his voice. Like he cared. About his reputation, though she was quite sure he didn't. About Ascione, though she hadn't been sure there was any loyalty there considering he'd had very little to do with it all these years.

But she'd banked on the probability that somewhere deep down, all the talk of legacies she'd grown up with would have been instilled in him as well.

"You'll marry me then." She managed to sound calm, but inside she was a nervous wreck. Inside, she was *praying* he said yes. And somehow dreading that yes at the same time. It was what she knew needed to happen, but it was not what she *wanted*.

And that really was the story of her life, so she couldn't fathom why it unsettled her as much as it did.

"Marry you? I thought you were brilliant, *cara*. Why would I have met you in public, for many to see, if not to plant the romantic seeds of our engagement?"

She could not stop herself from pulling a face at the word *romantic*.

Luciano chuckled. "You will need to work on your acting skills."

"Indeed." She cleared her throat. "But, if you did not notice the papers this morning, I have already planted my own seeds."

He did not frown exactly, but she could tell he had not gotten wind of the stories yet. She pulled her phone out of her purse and brought up one of the gossip channels that had the picture she'd arranged. Then she slid the phone across the table to him.

He picked it up. "Look at you, Serena," he murmured, studying the picture. He handed her phone back, then smiled, his gaze sharp and on her.

A flutter centered in her chest. Like nerves, but warmer. She felt…compelled to hold his gaze, even as something shifted low in her stomach. She didn't understand it.

Or like it.

Because as much as she'd like to pretend it was some kind of victorious feeling from having him agree to her plan, she knew it had nothing to do with agreement, and everything to do with that smile and his eyes on hers.

He lifted his glass of wine. "Then I suppose we have a deal. Let the games begin, *compagna*."

Partner.

She thought about how he'd said his father should be rotting in hell and hoped for a brief moment her father was doing the same for leaving her to deal with *this*.

They had agreed their first public appearance would be the dinner party put on by one of the CEOs of the major American conglomerate that had been swooping in and stealing their clients away.

As Luciano prepared himself for the dinner, he thought back to their parting shots to one another at lunch.

"I should like to see you in a color. Perhaps a hint of skin," he had said, to see if he could watch closely enough for her mask to slip.

It hadn't.

"I cannot fathom why you would care at all what I wear," she had replied as they'd walked back to his car.

"There should be some sense that we are rubbing off on one another, should there not?"

"Then what will you do?" she'd asked, sounding sincere. She'd delivered the blow with that same tone. *"Learn to read?"*

He had been torn between shocked affront and a laugh. She was indeed a worthy adversary. Except, no longer an enemy. Now, they were partners.

He wondered how long it would last before one of them would plan a betrayal.

Not until both companies were back on even footing. Serena would not risk Valli, and while he wasn't quite so taken with Ascione, he wanted none of his father's failures associated with his own name.

Because I am better.

So for a few months yet, they would have to be full-on partners. No behind doors backstabbing just yet.

What a shame.

In the days between their lunch and the dinner, he sent her flowers to her office. An outrageously large and overly bright combination that he knew would embarrass her.

And that would be the talk of the Valli offices.

It amused him to imagine it. Just as it amused him to

recall their lunch. And the different Serena's he'd come across in such a short time, after only ever seeing the perfect ice princess for so long.

But it was clear, she was not perfect. There was a strange hidden woman underneath the surface. There was something sharper there too, that he brought out when he irritated her enough. It poked at something deep within him, something he hadn't figured out quite how to articulate to himself. So he kept poking, waiting for clarity.

He could not recall a time he'd ever been so fascinated to see what made a woman tick, but then again, when women shared his company, they generally *wanted* to, with little reason to hide themselves away.

It was a marvel, and while the idea of being connected to her in any way, especially beyond business, was of course an atrocity, he was certain her plan would work.

She was that good at embodying a lie. How else had he spent all this time thinking her perfect, only to find her in thick-lensed glasses and octogenarian shawls surrounded by *cats*?

So when his driver stopped in front of Serena's home, Luciano did not hold on to any worries. The dinner party would be beyond mundane, and pretending to care about Serena's needs would be an odd experience, but he had no doubts they'd be successful.

He stepped out and studied the castle—it could only be called a castle—in the falling light of dusk. It was not elegant. There was no sense that this was an abode of luxury, though the inside *was* luxurious. But the outside gave more the aura of centuries long gone, when life was weary, bloody battle after weary, bloody battle.

This was a battle—though hopefully not bloody—so maybe the mood of it fit. He strode up the heavy set of concrete stairs that wound around, not romantically, but practically, and up to the main doors. He noticed what he could not have last night in the dark. There were hints of color here and there. A pot the color of the sea full to brimming with red and orange blooms to one side. A colorful stained glass trinket hanging from a hook that tinkled in the breeze along with the sounds of waves in the distance. A full awning of weeping wisteria shaded the entry.

He knew now that these were all glimpses into the *real* Serena, and he wondered…would he catch a glimpse of her now? That owlish little creature trying to pretend to be a lioness.

No, she'd be ready this time. He had no doubt. And he had the oddest sense of disappointment at that.

The door opened before he'd even stepped forward, and the man who'd argued with him that Serena was not to be seen the last time he'd been here answered.

His expression was grave. His eyes were wary. He gestured Luciano inside.

Luciano smiled charmingly at him when he said nothing. *"Buonasera."*

"Ms. Valli will be down momentarily, Mr. Ascione. You may wait here."

Luciano looked around the entry way. It was grand, indeed, but hardly the place to sit and wait. Luciano doubted very much that the typical visitor was asked to stand in the bright white room and *wait*.

But before he could suggest that, Serena appeared. She

was walking at a quick clip, checking the contents of her purse as her high heels clicked against the stone foyer floors.

There was no denying Serena was beautiful. Even in her ridiculous pajamas and alarmingly large glasses the other night, one could not deny that there was something *within* her that glowed, that enticed.

The business version of Serena was always sleek, elegant and…demure, he supposed, was the best descriptor.

But there was something…altogether different this evening.

She wore color. A vibrant, gleaming green. She…sparkled. He didn't think that would have caught him off guard all on its own. He was used to glittering, brightly dressed women. It was the brevity of that skirt, and the surprisingly long, lean legs now viewable because of it, made all the longer by the gold heels she wore.

Worse than the surprise was the awkwardly potent bolt of lust that fisted inside him. Unexpected and unwanted. Because lust was usually quite welcome, easily dealt with. He did not find himself attracted to women he had no intention of having.

And there was certainly no appeal to having Serena Valli.

She looked up absently. *"Buonasera,"* she offered, but her gaze was moving to her butler. "Pierro, you'll make certain Kate gets her medicine with her food this evening?"

"Of course."

She nodded, as if that settled that, and Pierro drifted out of the room with one last disapproving look in Luciano's direction.

Luciano would have asked her who the hell Kate was,

but her hair was pulled up, and wisps sprang free in lazy curls. Her hazel eyes were painted dark, which somehow brought out the flecks of green and gold in them. Her lips were bright, which showed off just how full they were.

It wasn't that she looked any different than she usually did in the grand scheme of things, particularly considering the neckline of the dress was high, the sleeves long. It was just that she was portraying herself in a style that made her look like anyone he might have on his arm.

It twisted some signals inside of his brain. Because he could admit she was attractive, but he could not admit he was *attracted to* her. She'd put on a costume of sorts, but he could not allow it to trick him.

She was a snake.

"Is everything all right?" she asked, cocking her head slightly, making the gold earrings dangling from her ears catch the light and refract it.

"Of course," he said, sounding so stiff he barely recognized his own voice. Unacceptable. "You look different."

She glanced down at herself. "I suppose I do. You were right, an admission I don't make lightly. But wearing color, looking more like someone you would usually have on your arm, will be far more gossipworthy than if I dressed as I usually do. Just as the hideous flowers you sent me did."

It was disorienting, to mix business with fake pleasure. That was all. He just had to get his wits about him. He put on his usual smile—always so easy—offered his arm and felt somewhat reassured when she hesitated.

It was still the same Serena underneath this costume, and he'd need to remember that to make it through the evening.

CHAPTER FOUR

SERENA WAS A bundle of nerves on the inside. On the outside, she was a fortress of sophistication. But taking Luciano's arm was like one final step into a madness she did not want, but had no choice about.

So she wasn't *eager* to start this farce.

She did not care for the dress. It left her feeling exposed, when usually her wardrobe, hair and makeup felt like armor. Today, it was simply a costume. A role she was playing.

A woman foolish enough to be caught up in the charming smile of Luciano Ascione. Because this was the element she *was* nervous about. How did one pretend to be in love with a man they hated?

And yet *hate* wasn't quite accurate as she put her arm in his. Something *else* was happening inside her body. It wasn't disdain. It wasn't revulsion. She had been in a male-dominated business enough to know what *disinterest* felt like.

This wasn't that, and she could not make sense of it since she did not like Luciano Ascione and never would.

Never.

He led her outside, and the cool air felt good against her

overwarm skin. The act of *walking* helped take her out of her tumble of thoughts and focus. Because everything in business was focus. One step and then another.

And any inner feelings—good or bad—did not matter.

He led her to his car and opened the door for her, and she did not make eye contact. She had been haunted for too many nights about what it felt like in that restaurant to meet his gaze.

She wanted nothing to do with it.

Once seated in the back of his car, she closed her eyes for a moment. Just to center herself. Just to remind herself what this was for.

"Nervous?"

"Of course not," she said, reacting too quickly, too forcefully. She knew it the minute she nearly jumped a foot out of her seat when Luciano put his large hand over her clasped ones in her lap.

She wanted to scoot farther away from him, but he was hardly crowding her. Even his hand came off hers quickly. There was absolutely no reason to find the spacious backseat too small. Too enclosed. And smelling far too much of his expensive cologne, something woodsy and enticing. Subtle, when the man was anything but.

"I suppose I am nervous," she said to him, because claiming the emotion she felt was the first step in defeating it. In maybe eradicating this winded feeling. "You are the experienced actor in this little play."

"Then let me do the talking."

"Talking, I am good at. I am not good at…" She trailed off, because she didn't know how to articulate it. She was always playing a role, so it wasn't that. It was simply that she usually played a role she chose, or maybe it was less of a role, less of a fiction, and more of a mask over her real self. One that suited her. Businesswoman. Whether it required a little flirting and ridiculous compliments, or shrewd no-nonsense facts. She could do it all.

But she did not know how to attend an event and pretend that it was simply to enjoy the company of her date. The goal was not business—it was gossip and drumming up interest in *her*.

She had always preferred to be in the background, to let the business do the speaking. No one needed to know about her cats or what she liked to read or the name she had planned for the miniature dachshund she was *this* close to adopting.

Now, she was pretending to let everyone know something. Something she didn't actually want anyone to know, because being fake in love with Luciano was embarrassing. He was a notorious playboy, flirted with anything that moved. Everyone would look at her and feel *pity* for thinking she of all people would have won his loyalty.

"I'm waiting for you to confess something you don't think you're good at, Serena. Frankly, I did not think hubris one of your main qualities."

She scowled at him. "One does not need hubris when one is self-aware," she returned with a primness that steadied her. Because she was *prim*, and organized, and controlling and therefore *in control*. She knew her flaws. Understood them and tried to keep them under that same control.

But she hated to hand her own shortcomings to *him* on a silver platter. Even if they were partners, short term, they were long-term adversaries. And she knew, from having to deal with her parents her entire life, that letting adversaries into your inner thoughts, inner worlds, only lead to hurt.

She would not let this man hurt her. And maybe that was why his smile, his touch, upended her, the strange sensations they elicited. These were not the actions of adversaries. There was some warmth under it all, and she only knew how to fight her parents' frigidness.

"It is not so much that I think I am not good at something, but I do have some concerns that, even with this wardrobe choice, some people will question the likelihood of…an *us*. We do not have anything in common, except hating one another."

"I suppose you have not heard the concept of *opposites attracting*."

She sighed. Heavily. "Except a woman as smart as I am would not be foolish enough to be attracted to the opposite of everything she valued—truth, intelligence, loyalty. And so on."

"You would be surprised at the amount of *intelligent* women I have had in my bed, *cara*."

She hated that her cheeks heated, because she had no doubt he had said it for that very reason. So that she would have to fight any *imagining* of such a thing from happening in her head.

But it was far too easy to imagine. Perhaps she had never been in *anyone's bed*, but she enjoyed love stories. Reading them, watching them. She liked believing that for some, that kind of companionship, dedication, romance and, yes, enjoyable sex, was possible.

Even if *she* wasn't made for it. There had been no physicality in her life to make her believe she was. Even her grandfather, for all his kind points, had not been a hugger. Her parents somehow less so. She had grown up with such a lack of physical touch, she did not know how to be comfortable with the *idea* of it in her romantic life.

So the fact he was mentioning it, the fact she was even… *thinking* about it, jumbled up all her certainties and plans, and *that* could not be born.

"I would never be surprised by the amount of people in your bed, Luciano," she managed to say, hoping she sounded sophisticated and casual about the whole matter. "But I feel it imperative to remind you that for our purposes, in public you must refrain from behaving your usual way. Flirting with anyone in a skirt. Touching other women. The crowd must believe that you care for *me*, and that will require the great lothario of Italy to keep his eyes and hands to himself."

There was a beat of silence where she thought maybe she'd shocked him, or offended him or scored some kind of point. She would have felt triumphant and celebrated that, but he seemed to purr out his response.

"Ah, but not to *himself.* I will have to keep my eyes and hands on you. No?"

He asked this like a kind of dare, so she kept her placid smile in place and refused to blush as his dark eyes held hers. It felt like his hands were on her all the same.

Her heartbeat seemed to *tremble* there in her chest and, for a breathless moment, she could almost *imagine* just that. His hands on her. Skin to skin. Warmth to warmth. A physicality that only existed in her imagination.

But, good lord, not with *him*. That was ridiculous. They

would only ever have to pretend physical intimacy in public, like a hand hold. Perhaps a dance.

A brushing of bodies, of lips.

But no more. No *more*. Because this was a ruse, and she could not allow him to think he had some upper hand, like he no doubt wanted. Maybe he thought he was charming. Maybe he wanted her off balance and thought this was the way to do it—no doubt, he used his charm and innuendo as a weapon as easily as breathing. So that was it.

So she did not wilt. She would *not* look away. She would not allow him the upper hand, no matter how her heart seemed to riot there in her chest. So she didn't just *act* unaffected, she made sure to put him promptly in his place.

"I suppose you are right. *Me*. I know it will be a great challenge, testing your wherewithal deeply—something you are not accustomed to. But I will endeavor to have faith in you, Luciano. Sometimes the most challenging people only need someone to believe they are capable of them being better than they behave."

She kept his gaze the entire time. Watched as a chill moved through his expression, a sharp-edged anger he did not unleash. She had insulted him.

Good.

Luciano had agreed to this party assuming that Serena might be *annoying*, insulting and her usual bland self, but he had not expected her to challenge him in quite such a way.

He wasn't certain how to combat it just yet. He knew what *he* wanted to do. Seduce every woman in the room simply out of spite. She seemed to expect it of him anyway, and he had no doubts he could do it, more or less.

As if he needed her *belief* in his ability to be *better*.

Oh, he'd be better. His usual approach to any problem was to live down to whatever low expectations he could muster, then dig even lower. It suited him well. People underestimated him, and he succeeded around that. Then, if they had to come face to face with his successes, they'd easily brush it off as a consequence of his name.

But Serena's expectations were *so* low, he found himself challenged to rise above them. Because as much as they couldn't stand each other, they had the same goal. So why not beat her at her own game? Why not, for once, be the victor in plain sight?

He liked that idea quite a bit.

He had never had reason to play the besotted lover. In fact, he tended to discourage such…connection. He made certain the women he dated understood that he was not looking for a Mrs. Ascione. That there would be no *future*. That he was interested in fun and fun alone.

The women who agreed enjoyed his brand of fun. The women who did not agree were shut out. It was a simple approach that had not caused him any trouble yet.

This was far more complicated. But if Serena wanted a besotted fool, dedicated to her and her alone, for the press and the stories and the good of their companies, why not deliver?

Why not show her just how *good* he was? So all her barbs no longer had any heft. So *she* had to adjust *her* plans that no doubt included being completely in charge, because he was too dim, or too busy seducing women, to handle what needed to be handled.

No, he would be the fifty-fifty partner she did not want,

and he would make everyone in this silly room believe he was in love with her, so this plan went off without a hitch. And any hitches would be *her* fault.

They walked into the charming villa, brimming with flowers and people, all important and rich. Some clients. Some enemies. He smiled, greeted, a hand lightly placed on Serena's back to make it clear they had arrived together.

She was right about one thing. He was an experienced actor. He'd been playing a role all his life, he liked to think. At first, he'd stepped into roles to garner his parents' attention— so they'd stop gearing their slings and arrows at each other.

He'd worked to be the perfect student to show his father he was an intelligent and worthy heir. He'd worried over his mother and done everything to show her he could be the protector his father had not been for her.

Both had rejected him and his earnest tries, so then he'd done the opposite. It had suited him much better when it came to his father, to see disappointment and regret in the old man's eyes. To live down to low expectations.

It had been more…complicated with his mother. She had shut him out, rejected him. So that there could be no *living down*. He could only stop trying, and with that came a guilt he had never fully been able to untangle.

Something he did not wish to nor need to contend with when it came to business, so he shoved that thought aside and focused on Serena. There would be no living down, no guilt, because she meant nothing to him, no matter how interesting she'd turned out to be.

It didn't matter. Only playing his role mattered.

His hand slid lower, and it was strange to have to even pretend to see Serena in the light of a *woman*. Because she was indeed. In fact, if there weren't any history be-tween them, and she weren't so stuffy, he might have been tempted. She did make a pretty sparkling package.

When his hand drifted lower, pulling her closer, she went still and stiff. He had to bite back a grin. But then he just aimed it down at her. "Relax, *cara*," he murmured cheer-fully. "All eyes are on us."

Her mouth curved in a pretty approximation of a smile, even if he could tell she'd like to shoot daggers from her eyes at him. "Then we are getting exactly what we wanted," she replied, nodding at someone who called out a greeting.

They moved through the room, greeting people they knew, getting sucked into conversations where avid eyes watched Luciano's hand on her back, her shoulder or clasp-ing her own. Serena didn't *relax* into it exactly, but it was clear she was playing it up as best she could. He thought she was good enough to fool just about everyone else.

Eventually, they got hailed in different directions and were separated for a bit. Luciano talked to a very disap-proving member of his father's staff at Ascione, who didn't want to come out and *ask* what Luciano was doing holding hands with the devil's daughter but came close enough.

Luciano had just laughed it off, irritating the man and entertaining himself.

When a pretty woman he'd usually flirt with sidled up to him, he was polite. He smiled. But he did not lay on his usual charm. In fact, he should pretend to look for Serena. Pretend to be distracted by her. *That* would get this group talking.

But when he found Serena with his gaze, he did not have to pretend. She stood with Tomasso Bonetti—who had once been a very important customer at Valli but had lately taken up with the American conglomerate—their heads bowed together.

They laughed and Luciano frowned.

She was the one who'd come up with this ridiculous plan. She was the one who'd warned him off flirting with other women. And now she stood *laughing* with another man. Tomasso was a good decade older than Serena, but Luciano did not trust that sly smile of his.

He didn't even bother to excuse himself from his current conversation companion, because he'd forgotten about her entirely. He strode across the room and approached Serena, sliding his arm around her waist in an easy movement that had her stiffening.

"I shall have to steal Serena away," he said to Tomasso, a feral smile in place. "They're playing our song."

Serena didn't frown. Not with her expression. But it was fascinating to be able to read the frown underneath the pleasant smile. Especially when no one else seemed to. She made her excuses to the man she'd all but been drooling over and then allowed Luciano to pull her onto the dance floor, and no one even looked twice at her. No one acted concerned that *clearly* the little dent between her eyebrows meant she was a little frustrated.

Did anyone ever watch her face like this, see it smooth out, and know that she'd thought through the issue, decided to make it a positive?

Something threaded through him at the idea that he did, *only* he did. A kind of weight. He was a man who liked to avoid weights and complications, but he found himself wanting to hoard this one. To have it only ever be his.

"Very clever," she said to him as the music began and he pulled her into his arms. She sounded surprised and vaguely indulgent, like a nursery schoolteacher, and that poked his frustration with her flirting with that *stronzo* even higher. "Make it look as if there is jealousy. Excellent touch."

He made a noncommittal noise. "Perhaps, but I feel I must remind you of the little warning you gave me earlier this evening. It is a two-way street, you know. You can't be draping yourself all over another man."

Serena laughed, and the sound was surprisingly light, *frothy.* A sparkle that had a few heads turning. The women immediately turned to whoever they were with and whispered behind hands adorned with jewels.

The men lingered too much on the length of Serena's legs as they moved to the slow, string notes that filled the air.

Luciano had to remind himself not to scowl.

"Draping? That's rich." She shook her head, the earrings at her ears winking in the light. "No one expects *me* to flirt, and even if they suspected that's what I was doing, which I can assure you no one did, they would consider it harmless. I do not have an endless array of famous, public lovers, Luciano."

"No, indeed you do not." And since he was feeling inexplicably frustrated, something he might call *jealousy* if he didn't know better, he leaned into a scathing reaction. Into her and figuring her out so he stopped feeling this... unsettled thing. "In fact, you don't seem to have a whisper of *any.*"

She stiffened in his arms, and he knew he'd made a direct and interesting hit. She didn't like that pointed out to her.

"I am discreet," she said, with a little sniff and that prim, pompous tone she trotted out like a weapon.

"Discreet or a virgin?" he asked casually.

She tripped over his foot, but before he could maneuver them back into the simple dance, the sharp heel of her shoe found the top of his. She put her full weight on it, causing a shock of pain to erupt in his foot.

"Oops," she offered with mock contrition. "I *do* apologize. Would you like to end our dance early? Perhaps you want to put some ice on it?" She asked all of this with a sweetness that was fake as the day was long. "I am just so terribly clumsy sometimes."

He gritted his teeth as he glared at her. "I will somehow survive your clumsiness, *cara*." Survive it. Survive her. Use this farce as the start of a new direction for himself. He would win this battle of the wills, rather than withdraw, rather than obscure, rather than *hide*. He had uncovered little hints at something softer under the icy demeanor, and he wouldn't rest until he'd found them all.

So he smiled down at her and brought a hand up to tuck a curling strand of hair behind her ear, making sure his finger grazed her cheekbone.

He kept moving her on the dance floor even as her posture went rigid, her cheeks a fascinating shade of pink, and she could not hold his gaze.

Oh, she'd like to be immune to him, and there was something about that realization, that *determination*, that she wasn't that gave him a thrill. A sense of purpose and satisfaction that he hadn't allowed himself in some time.

A challenge, because while he would no doubt win her over, charm her, get under that cold demeanor, it would not be *easy*. Serena *was* brilliant, and different. He did not know anyone like her, and there would likely be surprises in store.

There was a strange little alarm bell in the back of his mind, a warning about getting in too deep, too involved, too *interested*.

But this was Serena Valli he was contending with. No matter the challenge, he would win.

He had no doubt.

CHAPTER FIVE

SERENA WAS EXHAUSTED. Pretending was a chore and she did not care for it at all, but it was necessary. She wasn't convinced all his *touching* was necessary, but she supposed it put forth the appearances she wanted, so she couldn't complain.

But her muscles would be sore tomorrow from all the tensing against the strange reactions his touch elicited inside of her.

She had been on a few dates, because it was expected of her to carry on *some* social life—and to prove to her father that she was not "defective," as he liked to say, and that she might potentially marry. But the men she'd chosen had been just like her. Contained. Careful. Obsessed with work, usually.

And her work had been everything, just like proving herself in school had been everything before that. Her father required perfection, and she met it. Over and over again. She liked clear goals, and she liked keeping people relegated to business because it made it easy.

So the *dates* never became *relationships*, and there hadn't been any since her father's death.

Still, even without much experience, she had been confident she could pretend to be in a romantic relationship because she read novels and watched movies.

But the reality of pretending was…exhausting. She hadn't expected that.

She wanted to lean into the seat, close her eyes, and sleep the whole way home, but Luciano was still right next to her, and she didn't dare sleep in the presence of a scorpion.

Once home, she would take the longest, hottest bath imaginable. She would sleep in tomorrow—something she only allowed herself once a week anyway. She had earned her lazy day tomorrow.

Thankfully, Luciano did not speak the entire drive back to her house. Nor did he put his hand over hers again. He sat in the other seat, and his quiet and stillness made her nervous. Like he was *plotting* something.

But she wasn't about to ask *what*. Maybe she'd think about it tomorrow, try to suss out what he thought he was up to. But not tonight.

The car pulled to a stop and Serena made a move to get out herself, but Luciano *tsk*ed. "Come, Serena. You know better."

"We do not need to pretend in my front drive in the dark."

"Doesn't your staff need to believe our little farce?"

She opened her mouth to argue with that, but she had decided before this that of course they did. She wasn't sure she could pull one over on Pierro. He'd been the caretaker of this castle and its inhabitant since her father had been a child. He knew her too well.

But if everyone else fell for it, he would pretend he did not know it was fake. He would go along with it.

But she hadn't thought about how that would…*look*. In her private life. She'd been focused on how to make the public believe they were a couple.

He was opening her car door for her now, offering his hand to help her out. She didn't want to take it, pretend or no, but she had to. Just another curse to lay on her father's memory, she supposed.

Luciano kept her hand in his as he closed the car door behind her. Then he walked with her. Toward the castle. His large hand enveloping hers. Warm and strangely rough, when she would have expected his hands to be as smooth as the rest of him.

They walked up the stairs to the main doorway. Her heart tripped over itself in something like nerves. She wasn't *nervous*. She was just…uncomfortable. He was only walking her to her door. Like a good date would. She would turn, offer her cheek perhaps? She didn't *want* to feel his mouth on her, her hand, her cheek, her…

No, she didn't want to know what that felt like. Just the thought made her jittery and sick to her stomach. Maybe that jittery feeling was more like a free fall on a roller coaster than any kind of revulsion, but she was certain it came from not wanting to do it. Excitement wouldn't feel like this, so untenable and shaky. Besides, any *excitement*, would be a betrayal of her own self.

So it couldn't be that.

But some sort of physical good-bye was *necessary*, she told herself firmly as they reached her door. She turned to him, pulled her hand away, almost having to resort to tugging for it to be free. Once it was, she knew she had to give a little more. Pretend for the staff, as he'd said. She tilted her head, offering her cheek. A chaste kiss on the cheek was something she was going to have to get used to. So why not start now with only the audience of his driver and possibly someone looking on from inside?

But as he leaned forward, closer and closer, those dark eyes intense and on *hers* so that it felt like a touch in itself, her breath seemed to catch there in her throat. She couldn't inhale or exhale as his mouth brushed against her cheek.

Lightly, almost friendly. Certainly not *romantic*. But his breath on her skin was an intimacy she hadn't considered, and she didn't like the way it shivered through her. How it elicited wants that clearly had not originated in her *brain*.

She needed this to be over. She needed to be alone. To regroup. To… To… *Something* away from him.

"Good night, Luciano," she said, sounding polite and warm, she hoped, but it was hard to tell with the buzzing in her ears.

That intensified when she opened the door and he did not turn around and walk back to his car. He followed her into the warmly lit entryway.

"What are you doing?" she demanded, rounding on him as if she could protect her space from him physically.

"Coming inside," Luciano replied breezily.

"I did not invite you inside." She knew she sounded shrill. She could *hear* it, but she couldn't stop it.

"Quite the failure on your part. You *should* invite me in for a drink. And then we *should* retire to your room."

She could only gape at him. He wasn't actually suggesting…

"We are to make a splash, are we not?"

A splash?

He was mad. "I don't see what that has to do with you following me inside against my wishes. With you…" She couldn't say the rest. A drink was one thing. Her *room*?

"What better splash than a tabloid photo of my car leaving your home early in the morning? The speculation will run rampant."

The thought of him in her *home* overnight was…horrible. Absolutely terrifying. Maybe the fear she'd felt before had been heavy with claws, and this was light and fizzy. Maybe this felt more like a drink of champagne than any threat. The idea of him in her room, the idea of him…

She could not let her mind traverse down that road. It felt imperative to shut the door on any imagination there, before it…changed something.

A smart woman did not walk roads or have sleepovers—no matter how fake—with creatures who could sting. "You cannot spend the night here."

"Admittedly your crumbling castle is not my first choice in accommodations. Perhaps next time you can spend the night at my estate. With running water."

"I have running water. I have every amenity—" She stopped herself from continuing to defend her *home*, particularly in that horrible screech that made her want to wince. He was no doubt just trying to get a rise out of her. She inhaled, put all her armor back in place and smiled sweetly at him. "And I wouldn't stay at your estate if held at gunpoint, *carissimo*."

"Then I guess you are not as serious about this endeavor as I'd thought you were." He *tsked* lightly.

She finally understood the meaning behind the saying "seeing red." "I am more serious than you can *imagine*, Luciano."

"Perhaps you are. Perhaps you are just that out of touch with reality. You do realize a modern couple shares a bed before the wedding? Or does your choice of accommodations allow you to believe it is the year 1500?"

She hated that he could make her blush. That he should keep talking about *beds* and that whole thing about her being a virgin.

How could he *tell*?

It didn't matter.

"*We* will not be sharing a bed. Ever."

"No," he agreed so easily it made her want to stomp her foot like a child. "But people must think we are."

"So you intend to spend the night in my room?"

He shrugged. "Unfortunately, I do not see any way around it."

"You're *mad*," she shot at him as her heart rattled around in her chest, and a heat she couldn't seem to control crept into her cheeks. Because it was embarrassing to even consider. Embarrassing that people would think they were...

Embarrassment was the only explanation for this heat, for this skittering pulse inside of her. She didn't know what else it could be. Refused to consider anything but humiliation.

Everything about this was a disaster.

"I seem to recall this being your idea," Luciano said blandly. "In fact, I seem to recall you coming to my office and proposing to me."

"Yes, but—"

"Then, take me to your bedroom, *cara*."

* * *

Luciano hadn't really planned on enjoying himself. But it took no effort at all to have her spluttering and red-faced. When for as long as he'd known her, she'd been an icy, impenetrable wall. He'd gotten a little peek behind it that first night he'd come here, but only the polish. Now, he was seeing an actual unraveling, not just a pair of glasses.

Who knew all it would take was a fake relationship, a kiss on the cheek and some suggestion of *beds* to break through her perfect mask?

But she would not be Serena Valli if she did not know how to rein herself in and carefully put that mask back in place. Her chin lifted, her eyes flashed, but other than that her expression was perfectly bland.

He found himself completely fascinated by this change. By the way she could wield such strength of character. It made him want to unwind it, again and again, perhaps even in unwise ways.

"Follow me," she said briskly, then stalked out of the entry and deeper into her strange house. There were narrow, dark hallways, tiny windows that hinted at little light, and only when they reached the third floor did he realize she must have taken him through the back of the castle that was no doubt originally built for an array of medieval servants. Because the part he had been shown through the other night had been bright, opulent and cozy.

He wondered if it was a purposeful attempt at a slight— no doubt, really, when it was Serena doing the slighting. It amused him, in spite of himself. The little swipes she could take at him that she would no doubt deny.

Like stomping on his foot during their dance.

It did not fully make sense to him that he was enjoying her sparks of defiance. Perhaps because he'd once thought her blandly above such emotion.

Once at the top of the staircase, she led him down what would be a brighter hallway in the light of day since one wall was dotted with windows. The hallway was short, and only led to one door.

With the slightest of hesitations no one would have noticed if not looking for it, Serena pushed the door open. She flipped on a light, and he followed her into the room.

It was big and bright. One wall seemed to be made entirely of glass, and he could not make out the entire view it gave since it was dark outside, but there was water below. Right now, all he could see was a brightly shining moon and pretty starlight.

There was a truly spectacular ornate bed against one wall. Four posters, an array of comfortable looking and colorful blankets and pillows. He found himself transfixed by the idea of cold, uptight Serena cozying into that warm, cuddly bed.

But Serena did not look at the bed. She marched over to a door, jerked it open and stepped inside what appeared to be a very large closet. She reappeared, a little stack of folded clothes in one hand, before she crossed over to yet another door. The bathroom, he imagined.

She said nothing, just disappeared behind this door and firmly shut it behind her. He heard the *snick* of the lock being engaged and laughed.

He took in the rest of the room. It was an interesting combination of softly romantic art, brightly colored and patterned textiles, a bold view of the world outside her castle and…animal paraphernalia. There was a row of portraits—cat and dog faces, all painted up to look like kings and queens and military generals of a sort.

What on earth…?

He recalled the little fluff of a cat that had been in her sitting room the other night as something streaked out from underneath the bed and took a swipe at his shoelaces, then disappeared again. For a moment, he could only stare at the space where a cat's paw had just been. Before it crept out once more.

Luciano took a step away and then another. He could not quite get a read on Serena's private, interior life. Cats. Books. A homey kind of…grandmotherliness when the woman wasn't a day over twenty-eight, perhaps even younger, if he remembered correctly. A direct contrast to the sharp, modern businesswoman she presented herself as.

And he wondered what caused such a dichotomy. Perhaps he pretended to be less determined and hardheaded than he was, but he did not hide key elements of his personality away.

What would make a person do such a thing? What did it mean? Why did it all come together like a story he was desperate to know the ending to?

The door reopened and Serena stepped out. She was dressed casually now, but he didn't think there was anything casual about the way she was covered from head to toe. A soft sweatshirt that had a mock turtleneck. Pants that were utterly shapeless and looked equally soft. And thick socks. The only skin he could see was her face and her hands.

"There is a cat under your bed," he told her.

"There are likely two cats under my bed," she replied. "It's one of their favorite places." She looked up at him then. "I don't suppose you're allergic?" she asked.

Hopefully.

"Not to my knowledge."

For the first time since he'd stepped inside her house, she smiled at him. "You could rub your face in one and find out."

"I shall abstain, I think."

She shrugged, but the smile stayed in place. "Let me know if you change your mind." She said nothing else and didn't move from her spot all the way across the room from him. She just stood there, offering nothing into the silence.

Except what he could only define as a nervous energy. She held herself perfectly still, her expression placid. But there was a tension *wafting* off of her, and Luciano could not lie. He enjoyed having that effect on her.

Any affect, really, that chipped through what he'd once thought was impenetrable ice.

So he took a few steps in her direction, grinning when she took the same amount of steps in the opposite one.

He stopped, regarded her across the room with a raised eyebrow. "What exactly are you afraid of, Serena?"

The look of outrage chased across her face. "I am not *afraid*."

"You locked the bathroom door like I'm the big bad wolf. You stand across the room like I might bite."

"I locked the bathroom door because that's what you

do when you go into a private area that you wish to remain private."

"Do you think I'm going to burst in and pounce upon you?"

"Of course not. Don't be ridiculous." But her face was getting redder and redder, like now that he'd introduced the words *bite* and *pounce* she could picture it all too well.

Which had him considering what that picture would look like. What it might be like to cross the room and—

Before he remembered himself. Who he was. Who she was. What *this* was. A farce.

But that did not mean he could not enjoy a farce. As long as he remembered himself. Which had never been a problem before.

Why should it be a problem now?

"This is a large bed. I suppose it shall do for our purposes." He moved over to it now, eyed the bed skirt for any evidence of paws, then decided to leave his shoes on. He settled himself on the bed in a sitting position, crossing his ankles over a bright purple coverlet of some kind and lacing his fingers behind his head against the padded headboard decorated with images of tiny…pigs?

For a moment, he wondered if he'd given her a kind of stroke. She stood utterly still, her mouth hanging open ever so slightly, no noise coming from it.

Eventually, she blinked, as if coming back into herself. "I am hungry," she declared, reaching for the door.

"As am I. Have a tray brought up. I'm not picky about food. If you have any good liquor, I wouldn't mind a drink as well."

"You are not… We are not…" She spluttered on some

more without actually articulating a word. It was fascinating. He had never seen her struggle to undercut a man—any man, including himself—with an icy smile and perfectly sharp words.

She didn't stutter. She didn't falter. She was the kind of woman who showed up at a man's club and suggested they *marry* to save businesses and legacies.

But slowly, she brought it all back. She took a deep breath. She closed her eyes for a moment. There was a whole process of resetting herself, and he watched it happen in front of him.

Fascinating. What must it be like to have that inside a person?

"I have considered your point," she said, in that prim, controlled voice of hers. "You are somewhat correct that any engaged couple should be considered to be…cohabitating at times. If we arrange someone to photograph and leak said photograph of you leaving here early in the morning, we'll get a lot of traction from that."

"That might even be why I suggested it," he returned dryly, still lounging on her bed that smelled crisp and reminded him of spring.

She ignored his sarcasm. "That being said, we must consider our own comfort while we engage in this little facade."

"I am quite comfortable."

She inhaled through her nose this time.

"I am not. I am used to having my space to myself. I am used to a certain level of…" She paused, searching for a word, though she was back to her normal self, not faltering. Just being careful. Precise. "Solitude. It is my preferred state of being. So, perhaps we should use this time together to fully iron out an agreement."

"An agreement?"

"Yes. We don't want to go the route of full legal contract just yet, as that could be leaked. But an agreement between the two of us. How we will proceed, behave. Lay out expectations."

"Expectations."

"Are you struggling with the meaning of the words themselves or something else?" she asked, smiling sweetly. But no amount of masks could hide the annoyed snap in her tone.

"I find myself baffled by the way you speak."

"I will try to dumb down my vocabulary to meet you where you are."

She said this almost kindly. Luciano smiled mildly at her. He did not defend himself to anyone. He'd learned from a young age there was no point, and it usually worked in his favor to be underestimated.

But her comments grated all the same, and he had to remind himself that there was a larger game at play then this inconsequential conversation in her bedroom.

"Well, by all means. Let us iron out an agreement. But have some food and drink sent up first. God knows I'll need one to get through this."

CHAPTER SIX

SHE HAD INDEED had food brought up, and a bottle of scotch. Though Serena had moved to take the tray herself, Luciano had swept in and smiled charmingly at Pierro, who had uncharacteristically delivered the tray himself.

It had been clear he hadn't wanted to relinquish the tray to Luciano and that he was…checking on her, she supposed. But she'd smiled and inclined her head, a nonverbal *Give him the damn tray*.

Just so this could all be over with.

Luciano had taken it, closed the door rather pointedly, then taken it over to the bed. He'd poured himself a glass, made himself up a plate of the elegant snacks, then settled himself back into her bed.

Her *bed*. She knew he did it to annoy her. Perhaps even to shock her. So she was working very hard to pretend like it didn't matter.

But it grated. The way his long body made her large, soft bed look small. The way that it was now too easy to picture him there, where she *slept*. It brought to mind the books she loved to read where a couple who hated each other were stuck at some inn somewhere with one bed. And the end result was always…

Well, she was *not* going to think about that right now. Not with *him* in *her* bed.

Since he'd taken the bed, and she had no intention of being anywhere near him, even if she *was* hungry, she settled herself at her desk. She opened the drawer that held her notebooks. For this endeavor, she'd chosen one decorated in scorpions. An apt reminder. While she liked to use a variety of colorful pens in her note-taking, for the Valli-Ascione merger she used a scathing black. She'd drawn a little cover page with her own rendition of scorpions, snakes and rats with red eyes. It made her chuckle every time she opened it.

A necessary levity in this otherwise nightmare endeavor, that only seemed to become more nightmarish as time went on.

She began to flip the pages until she found the first blank one. She smoothed out the paper, letting the act soothe her. Any difficult problem could be solved if she put pen to paper. This had always been true, and she refused to acknowledge this problem might be too complex and fraught.

She would find a way. She labeled one side of the page *Expectations* and the other *Rules*. She was so intent on writing each letter precisely so it would be aesthetically pleasing, a physical representation of the perfection she sought, that she did not notice Luciano had gotten up and come to stand behind her.

Until he spoke, making her jump and accidentally draw a harsh line across the corner of the page.

"What is this?" he asked.

"My notes," she replied, staring at the ugly line. Ruining her perfection. Just like *him*. Because of course Luciano Ascione had never had to be perfect.

"On paper?"

"I find I think best when I can write everything long-hand," she replied loftily. Later, when she was blissfully alone, she would rip out this ruined sheet and rewrite all her notes quite carefully. But for now, she would have to make do.

"You are a far stranger creature than I could have ever given you credit for, Serena."

She did not like the way he said her name. He seemed to linger on the consonants, drawing it out. Unnecessarily, in her estimation.

She was tempted to write under rules, *Do not say my name*. But that was ridiculous and petty.

Perhaps in the back, when he wasn't here, she'd make a ridiculous and petty list. Just for her own amusement.

For now, she would focus on building the scaffolding she needed to survive this without resorting to violence.

"I feel it should go without saying, and I'm sure you were just *jesting* before, but obviously we will not share a bed."

"Metaphorically or literally?"

She gritted her teeth at the silky way he spoke. No doubt it worked on whatever targets he actually wanted to talk into bed, but when it was aimed at her, it just felt like… Something sharp and confusing. He was jumbling her up purposefully, but she felt out of her depth because she did not understand this kind of…jumble.

"Both." Then, in her precise, careful script, she wrote it down.

Will not share a bed—literal/figurative.

When he snorted, she did not *glare* at him. She moved down to the next line and wrote the number two.

"Number two, I should think, would be to not flirt with a CEO in the camp of our enemies."

She could not understand why he kept harping on that. "There is professional flirting and then there is private flirting. One is necessary, and no one will think twice about it. Particularly coming from me." She'd never considered it flirting so much as…stroking the male ego. And none of the businessmen she'd encountered had ever taken it as more than that.

Perhaps Luciano did not understand this because he was so handsome and charismatic, because he wanted that kind of attention. Men simply did not look at her that way and she knew it was a combination of how she handled herself and how little…*spark* she had. Her mother had been explaining that to her since she'd been a child.

"Is this so? You will have to explain to me the difference between professional flirting and personal flirting."

She sighed. No doubt all the flirting *he* did was meant to lead to the bedroom, so he could not understand the fine art of *actually* doing business. Wooing clients. Soothing concerns. "Professional flirting is like manners. No one thinks it's leading anywhere. It's…friendly. A little ego boost for the party who needs it."

"And how is this magically construed as different than *private* flirting?"

"It's simply part of the *professional* interaction. No direct invitations made." She looked down at the paper rather than him *looming* over her. "Private flirting is probably anything *you* do," she muttered irritably. She'd seen him do it. Maybe he'd dialed it down at the event, *pretended* to aim all that charm at her instead of the kind of woman he usually had on his arm.

And thinking of that frustrated her, because she understood just how potent and effective it could be if you believed in an Ascione scorpion.

Luckily *she* would not. She was too smart to think a little flutter, a little eye contact that had her pulse scrambling, mattered. Even if she could still feel all those things right now.

"Perhaps you could be more specific?" He was closer then, somehow, and he lifted her to her feet by the elbow, then turned her so that they stood face to face. Then he smiled. And it didn't look like *malice*. It looked like intent, which even she knew was different.

Not that she trusted it.

"Show me," he said, his hand still cupped there on her elbow, and even though she was wearing a sweatshirt she could *feel* the heat of his palm through the fabric.

She found herself having to swallow in order to speak. He was toying with her, and she had prepared herself for all the ways he might test her, but she hadn't counted on… this, she supposed. She knew she was smarter, more determined, far more professional than this man, but he knew how to zero in on the things she was not confident in.

Mainly…this strange magnetic pull. She could not call it *charm*, because she was not *charmed* by him. It was something darker, more illicit. Seduction…but at least she knew it was only meant to embarrass her. She had no *interest* in him, nor he her, so it wasn't as though she was afraid something untoward might happen. More…

She simply did not know how to box it up, control it,

undercut it. She could not seem to control her body's odd, unfamiliar responses. Frustrating, but not the end of the world. She would learn.

Serena *always* learned.

"It is not anything that requires a demonstration," she told him, using her best haughty managerial voice. She did not jerk her arm away, no matter how much she wanted to. In a test of wills, she would always, *always* win. But she did not dare look directly into his dark, amused eyes. She fixed on a strand of dark hair that swept across his forehead. "Laughing at a terrible joke, complimenting someone. These are all harmless flirtations. Business flirtations. Private flirting involves touch. The brush of a hand. Knees touching under a table. It is *physical* and promises something physical in return."

"So, what you are saying is, for our audience to believe in our little fiction, we must engage in the promise of something physical?" He let that sit there between them. A silence that settled in her throat like some kind of blockage, as his mouth curved ever so slightly, the look in his dark gaze downright piratic. "In public, that is," he added, with a feigned innocence that did not suit the *scorpion* tail in his smile at all.

Or the way his hand moved from elbow to waist. Curled there, in a strangely possessive touch. And for a moment, that touch—not at all different from when they'd danced tonight and she'd been wearing much *less*—seemed to do something to drain all the thoughts from her brain.

Which, she thought, was the *point*. And if she could focus on the fact he was playing some kind of... *Luciano*

Ascione game with her, she would not be felled by…whatever this was.

"I suppose, if you think it necessary." It irritated her that her voice sounded *lower*, but she did not let it show. "But you know what else would suffice?" she replied, pleased with her cool tone this time, even if she could feel the heat on her cheeks betraying her.

"What?"

"A ring. Expensive. Gaudy." She held up her left hand, wriggled the ring finger. "For all to see." She carefully dislodged herself from his grasp, because she didn't know how much longer she could hold on to that *detachment* when the feel of him seemed to brand himself there on her skin.

No one could accuse her of scrambling away. For that she would be proud. She fixed him with an indulgent smile, meant to grate. "No public groping necessary."

"I have never been accused of *groping*, *cara*."

She made a considering sound, making it clear she didn't believe him without coming out and saying it. Then she settled herself back in her desk chair. "Now, what other rules should we commit to paper?"

She'd come up with ten more. Luciano couldn't even remember them. She yammered on like the most boring of school lecturers, and he'd settled himself on her bed where he'd determined he would sleep. If only to watch her splutter like an offended nun.

After she took what seemed like a million years to meticulously put away everything in her desk, she turned to him with that cool look, a small smile in place. "Now, we must discuss sleeping arrangements."

He didn't discuss it. He slept in her bed. He had offered to share it and enjoyed doing so. She had so icily declined, it had delighted him. Particularly when she'd stalked over to the closet, pulled out some linens, then made herself a little bed on the window seat. Her tiny demon cats had hopped up and made themselves comfortable on her blankets, blinking at him in ways that felt…threatening.

Which was ridiculous, of course. Neither of them were much bigger than his *hand*.

In the morning, he'd woken in her surprisingly comfortable bed to find her gone from the window seat. Any bedding she'd used had clearly been put away.

The man who seemed to run the staff had met Luciano in the kitchen when he'd found his way there and told him coolly that Ms. Valli was indisposed and that he was welcome to leave whenever he saw fit.

Reading between the lines, Luciano read that as *now*, but he'd taken the offered coffee instead, overstayed his welcome to all and sundry before waltzing out of the place and to his car.

In the midmorning light, Luciano drove back to his apartment in the city. He noted the photographer hiding in a curve of the drive up to Serena's home, but pretended he did not.

The stories would be abuzz in their circles by lunchtime. He would no doubt start hearing from his father's stalwart advisors who would love to oust him if they could figure out how.

This would certainly ignite their ire, but no one would be able to fault him for what this would do for the company. The attention would put their name in circles where the Americans had been dominating. It would have their on-the-fence customers interested enough to take meetings again.

Two wealthy people from families long known to be in a feud would indeed be gossip fodder. Not new to him, considering the company he tended to like to keep was very interested in press and any kind of publicity they could drum up, but it would be new to Serena.

In some ways, she had a far better plan than he could have come up with. And in other ways, he didn't think she had the slightest clue what she was getting herself into.

He supposed that dichotomy was why he had such a difficult time pushing thoughts of *her* away as he went about his day. It was the only possible reason, really.

Besides, what modern woman in their twenties kept a drawer full of colorful notebooks and markers and used them? What kind of young woman lived in a castle decorated with the strangest animal themes?

Pigs on her headboard. It was insanity.

He couldn't seem to stop thinking about it. About how the oddness suited her, interested him, *charmed* him. For all her attempts to be average and customary on the surface, she was anything but underneath.

As he arrived at Ascione, he told his assistant he would be indisposed until after lunch. To hold his calls, allow no one in. Then he'd let himself into his father's office.

His office.

He'd redecorated, finding it necessary to not spend his time in his father's oppressive style. Luciano didn't *mind* the heavy handed opulence his father employed like a power move, he simply didn't think it was necessary.

He much preferred everyone to underestimate him. So everything was simple. Expensive, of course, but sleek lines and minimalism as a direct contrast to his father's maximalism. It suited his purposes here and, even better, Luciano knew his father would have hated it. So there was satisfaction in that.

"I hope there is a view from hell," he murmured to the line of portraits on the wall. The one thing he hadn't been able to get rid of. The line of Asciones who had built this company, built the wealth he'd used as a jumping off point for his own. This row of bastards who'd treated everyone around them like a pawn or an enemy.

Because Luciano might have disdain for them all, but he knew he was one of them. He had tried to be good, noble. Tried to be a protector.

And never managed.

This was his legacy, his blood. Might as well remember it.

He moved for his desk, pushed away all thoughts that weren't next steps. He went over all the information Serena had sent his pretend man of affairs again. Her plan was thorough, but not complete. She was looking for stability. Shoring up foundations. The attention their union, their merger, would draw would be huge and it would no doubt win some of their lost customers back. But that was all she'd planned for. Getting the old back.

Per usual, he thought bigger. Not just setting themselves up for what they'd *had*, but destroying the American interlopers in the process and giving themselves the opportunity for more.

As she'd said the other night: billionaires never needed an excuse for wanting more.

So, in his own document, he used the foundation of her plan to make a bigger one. No doubt hers stopped short of *bigger*, because she had plans for what would happen *after*.

Once they vanquished their common foe, they would become enemies once again, even if they were legally wed. He would need to have a plan in place to come out on top *then*. She clearly did.

So, he would. But he would need some…subterfuge. A distraction. Last night had started the seeds of that plan, and going over all this, adding to it, made it clear—the only thing that would work against Serena was the one thing she was so sure wouldn't.

He would simply have to seduce her.

He ignored the troubling wriggle of doubt in the back of his mind, because it did not stem from *doubt*, but rather how little the prospect bothered him. It would be no hardship, because there was a bloom of *something* under all that ice. A fire he seemed well adept at bringing out.

That concerned him. His own physical reaction to it. A shade too eager for his liking. But that only required control, and he knew how to wield it when it was necessary.

Besides, if *he* felt it, so did she. He had never seen her falter, except the few times he'd managed to have his hands, no matter how chastely, on her.

She was innocent, clearly, but not immune. His biggest hurdle would be convincing her that one didn't need to *like* the other person for the physical match to be enjoyable.

So perhaps she was due a lesson.

CHAPTER SEVEN

SERENA DID THE laundry herself once he was gone. It was cathartic to strip the bed he'd *defiled* with his long, rangy body, to heft the entire basket of bedding down to the washer and dryer and handle it with her own two hands.

An exorcism of sorts. She would wash away the memory of waking up to him in her bed, sprawled out in *her* sheets, *her* duvet, *her*s. He had looked fierce, even in sleep, like some ancient conqueror. And she had sat there in her window seat, staring for far longer than she'd like to admit, wondering what it would have been like to have woken up *next* to him. To feel his body heat, his skin and all the ways her body reacted to those things.

She'd had to leave her own room, just to find her usually firmly in place common sense. She'd avoided any goodbye because she *knew* embarrassment would swamp her.

But now she'd washed him away and all would be well. She'd make sure of it.

Because the sheets had put her behind schedule, she'd decided to work from home. She had a few calls, lots of emails to respond to, but no meetings that required her in the office today, thank goodness.

During her lunch, she'd gone ahead and written out her

ridiculous and petty list as a fun little break. Maybe it was pointless as they were not rules she would enforce, or even show him, but it felt therapeutic to put all her wishes into the written word. Complete with stickers depicting donkeys in flower crowns.

Do not utter my name.

Do not touch me.

Do not look at me.

Do not enter my room, let alone even look *at my bed.*

It frustrated her that just writing down these things brought images to her mind. Remembered bodily reactions. A jump in her stomach, a throb too low to have a great excuse for. The way her skin seemed to flush at certain looks he gave her.

It frustrated her that even knowing what an absolute reprobate he was, he was handsome as a devil and knew how to use it against her. She liked to think herself better than such *base* reactions, but she supposed she could not fully fault her brain for what was simply a *physical* reaction.

Besides, he was a man who knew how to use the physical, and she was just not…used to that. She did not engage in such behaviors and gave a wide berth to anyone who did. The few men she'd gone on dates with had not made physical overtures. The last one had even asked permission before kissing her cheek good night.

She'd hated it. And hated herself for hating it. Because it had simply made it clear that she would have to settle for a future where she was truly and utterly alone. That even someone who might be *like* her didn't…match. Didn't allow herself any comfort.

Or worse, any excitement. Which she didn't *think* she was looking for. Didn't *want* to be looking for.

For the best, she often assured herself. Perhaps the castle could get a little lonely, particularly during long winter months when even work couldn't distract her from the fact there was not one person in the whole world who cared about her beyond what she could do for a company.

But it was better to be alone, to do exactly as she pleased without having to don all the masks required of trying to make someone like her. Or pretending to be swept away by someone who asked permission to *kiss a cheek*.

Luckily, she did not need to make Luciano like her. This wasn't a business deal that required dancing to the tune of the male ego. In public, perhaps she would have to pretend more than she'd ever pretended before, but at least behind closed doors she could let loose with what she really thought of him. It was…refreshing, actually. To just say what she thought. To just be herself and not *worry*.

She could be herself in every way, at least in private. So long as she did not let the strange *physical* reaction somehow win. So long as she found a way to stop him from playing these power games that left her feeling unsettled. So long as she did not engage in that so much that she forgot to keep an eye on whatever his counterplay would turn out to be. Because if *she* was thinking about what happened after they vanquished their common enemy, no doubt so was he.

She considered, yet again, the fact that he was allegedly posing as his own man of business. She was not *shocked* he might hide a keener mind than she'd like to give him credit for, but she did not understand why he'd hide it away. She'd refused to ask or even acknowledge it, because she thought that's what he expected of her.

Still, it sat there in her mind like an unsolvable puzzle. It made her wonder what else he might be hiding away. She had to be careful. Even if she'd underestimated him in the beginning, *maybe*, she'd known that she had to be careful. That this would not be straightforward or easy, and the upper hand would require constant vigilance.

Still, she worried she wasn't seeing the whole picture. She flipped pages back to the front of the notebook and went over her plan. Considered what she now knew about him and how he worked.

How had he built that club to the height of popularity?

Money, of course. No doubt using some of his father's contacts. But there had to be some business sense there. She'd watched him engage with people at the dinner party last night. He used *charm*. Compliments and smiles and easy jokes. He used the way he looked to dazzle.

But with her, he'd taken an opposite approach. He tried to make her uncomfortable. Innuendos about her bed. The way he'd said the word *bite*, when saying she acted afraid he might.

He wanted her flustered. Blushing and uncomfortable. And he undoubtedly thought it some special power he had, not just the fact that she was uncomfortable with the idea of…intimacy. He thought she was flustered by his handsomeness and insinuations.

He was most certainly wrong. Her discomfort last night had nothing to do with *him* personally. Nothing at all. She just wasn't used to a man in her space. That was all.

Confident with that interpretation of last night's events,

Serena gave herself a little nod and carefully put her note-book away. The plan that was taking shape was not one she could commit to paper now that he knew she liked to write things out.

No, this would have to stay in her head. Because she knew he'd proceed with her as he had last night. Charm-ing smiles, feigned innocence in his touches and threaded innuendo in everything.

This was how he would attempt to get some upper hand, no doubt. Continue to push her boundaries. Not just in the personal space of her home, but farther. Into her *actual* personal space.

Yes, he would certainly try to seduce her, and going into this, she hadn't really considered he might seriously. It was such a bizarre way to handle business, and she knew she was not the type he usually lent himself to. But it wasn't about what he *liked*. It would be about what he wanted.

Her knee-jerk reaction to this was obvious denial. If he so much as tried it, she'd cut him off at the knees. She would resist. Forever.

She *could* resist, if she wanted to. Curiosity wasn't the same as being unable to resist. Her imagination *sometimes* drifting his way didn't mean she wasn't smart enough to remember who and what she was.

And what he was.

But rejection was expected. What kind of power might she wield if she didn't react the way she usually did? What if she gave him the illusion of the upper hand? What if she *let* him seduce her?

The idea was appalling of course—that was the only thing the feeling in her stomach could be, because it certainly wasn't a jump of anticipation. That pulse scramble, that woozy feeling in the pit of her stomach, like when they'd locked eyes last night. Intrigue and interest as to what all that might lead to.

Nothing, Serena.

But he would assume he had all the control if she let him believe she was dazzled by his…physical prowess. If she let him believe she was foolish enough to be swept away by him, physically and maybe even romantically, he would think he had all the upper hands.

But really *she* would. If she went in with her eyes wide open. It would leave him open for a mistake—for lots of mistakes.

If she saw this as a business move, it wasn't lowering or embarrassing. It was simply what must be done to save her legacy. If she focused on *business*, she wouldn't worry that it might feel like…more.

Besides, maybe she wouldn't have to give in completely. Would he *really* try to take her to bed when he found her dull and frumpy compared to the beautiful women he surrounded himself with? That was a line even he wouldn't cross.

Besides, that was a problem for later. A cross-that-bridge-if-they-come-to-it situation. For now, she had to set up the first steps. The fake-falling-for-his-charm steps.

She pulled out her phone. Brought up a text to him and typed it out.

Dinner at seven, here at my castle.

She would couch it as a business dinner. She'd made some progress with the D'Angelo account, and she would apprise him of this. Along with a plan for him to dazzle the Franco team next week.

When her phone dinged, his response was obnoxious. Of course.

Where is the "please", amore mio?

She didn't bother to respond to that.

He would show up. And they would have a romantic dinner, discuss business and then she would let him flirt and push the boundaries and this time, she might respond. At least a little.

So the trap would be laid.

And if there was a little flutter of anticipation—no, not that. *Nerves*—well, she would master those as well.

Luciano was full of good humor as he drove up the twisting road to Serena's castle once again.

His assistant had dutifully collected all the stories about him and Serena this afternoon, and Luciano planned to go over them with her and discuss next steps in their "relationship" department.

He did not know what *she* had planned, but he had plans of his own beyond business. No doubt that would be the story of their strange partnership. A constant battle. Skirmishes lost and won. It was oddly…exciting. The prospect of clashing with a worthy adversary.

As long as he came out on top more than she did, he had a positive feeling about how this could end up.

She had definitely brought him a brilliant idea. He

would enact it even better than she could possibly imagine. Though whether she gave him any credit was doubtful.

Most of his challenges were done in private, where no one ever knew. It was best, always, for no one to truly know him. It allowed him to always accomplish what he set out to do. And while everyone attributed his success to *luck*, he knew the truth. How hard he'd worked. How much he'd overcome. And that no obstacle was too big for Luciano Ascione.

The knowledge had him whistling on his way up her staircase. He was let inside by the disapproving butler Luciano had yet to charm. He'd get there though. He always did.

"Ms. Valli has dinner waiting on the sea balcony," the man said stiffly, and then led him through the house. The back of the house, as Serena had last night. It amused him, these silly little slights.

Up a winding staircase and into a different hallway than last night, Luciano was led out a door and into the warm, breezy evening on a large balcony. Vibrant plants spilled from colorful pots. More strangely fanciful decoration popped out here. Wind chimes and all sorts of sculptures of animals in different mediums.

What *was* her obsession with animals? She made no sense. That feeling did not diminish when his gaze finally found her where she was standing at the curve of the railing, surveying him with those cool eyes.

Her expression was guarded, but the way she stood at the edge of the balcony was relaxed. And still… There was something about the way she held herself that made him wary. Was this the same woman who'd been frustrated to let him into her home last night? Smiling at him welcomingly now?

"Good evening, Luciano," she greeted.

He did not like the way she said his name. Something about it scraped along the back of his neck like a terrible portent melding with goose bumps. He had to fight off a scowl. What man got *goose bumps*? Certainly not *him*.

"Good evening," he offered, forcing himself to smile at her in the way that usually had her frowning.

She didn't frown today, though he did see the way her hand tightened briefly on the railing she rested it on before she relaxed it again. She gestured at the table. "I know this isn't visible like a restaurant might be, but the press was eating up your car leaving the hill this morning."

"Are you inviting me for another sleepover?"

Her mouth flattened, but she didn't scowl. She seemed to be making a great effort not to. She inhaled, then the corners of her mouth turned ever so slightly upward. "Whatever furthers our purpose," she said, with a kind of knowing that was almost…sultry.

Except this was Serena, so he was imagining things, surely. Still, it was clear something was off. He couldn't quite put his finger on the difference. She was dressed casually enough. The pants she wore looked soft and gave little hint at shape. She was not covered to the chin, he supposed, instead wearing a tank top the color of the sky at dawn, a pearly kind of blue. It was formfitting, but hardly skimpy. Still, he could see the shape of her arms, the freckles that dotted her shoulders as if she spent considerable time in the sun, which didn't seem true to the woman she was at all.

And now he knew that these details, like the long,

lovely shape of her legs, would be lodged uncomfortably in his brain.

He tried to look at it as a positive. Being attracted to her might be a bit of an affront considering she had always been his enemy, but it would make seduction enjoyable. Still, there was an uncomfortable tug of war going on inside of him, like there was a complication threading through all of this. It wasn't just business. It wasn't just seduction. It was layers—who they were because of their fathers, what they'd built themselves into, all the strange ways she fascinated him.

He did not care for *layers*. He preferred things to be… straightforward.

So he looked at the table between them, set for dinner. A bottle of wine in a bucket of ice, bruschetta displayed prettily on a colorful serving platter. It had every detail of a romantic, private dinner for two.

"I thought we should eat outside, then we can take a walk down to the beach. It's private, but an intrepid photographer with an excellent zoom lens should be able to catch sight of us from there."

"Smart."

"Besides, being outdoors means the stench of rat doesn't infect my dining room." She offered that sweet smile meant to slice a man to ribbons.

Ah, *there* was the Serena he expected. With a fiery orange sunset lighting her from behind, she looked a bit like a painting…

Vengeful Goddess at Sunset.

She only needed a bow and arrow or spear of some kind. Instead, she moved forward and lowered herself into a chair at the table. She lifted the bottle of wine and began to pour. When he did not immediately take a seat, she raised her gaze and an eyebrow at him.

He wasn't sure what was causing him pause, so he moved forward and took the seat across from her.

"Have you seen the stories?" she asked.

"Yes. They have bought into *us* hook, line and sinker."

Serena nodded, a wine glass in her hand as she gazed out at the water beyond the balcony. Her expression was thoughtful, and she did not sip from her glass. "I think we'll want to move quickly. No long, drawn out court-ships. We don't want the excitement to ebb. Just one story after the next."

He agreed with her, which shouldn't frustrate him as much as it did. He should be happy when they agreed. It would no doubt be rare, even with a common goal. But he hated the idea of her congratulating herself for her good ideas when he had them as well.

So he said nothing—not agreement or disagreement—as they ate in strangely peaceful silence. Like people who'd known each other long enough not to need to fill in those spaces.

When dessert was served, darkness had fallen except for fairy lights hung expertly, illuminating the balcony in something that felt like candlelight.

The *millefoglie* was delicious, the night lovely, the com-pany…oddly comfortable. But realizing how thoroughly he'd enjoyed an essentially silent dinner bothered him on a cellular level.

He stood. "Shall we take that walk?" he offered.

She sighed heavily. "Yes, of course." Reluctantly, she got to her feet. "I suppose we should talk about something."

She sounded genuinely and amusingly disappointed that they might actually have to have a conversation.

"I don't mind a silence now and again."

She snorted. "Come, Luciano. You have built a life in which you never have to live in the silence of your own thoughts. It is much talked about how much time you spend at that club of yours."

She was not completely wrong. Up until his father's death, he had always sought to drown out the thoughts, the feelings by throwing himself headlong into his club, into the women there.

But something happened when his father died. He supposed it was a kind of natural understanding that he himself would not live forever. He too could do something stupid tomorrow and end up a mangled mess on a cliffside.

Luciano wanted to be something more than his father had ever allowed him to be. So, in an effort to reacquaint himself with Ascione and deal with the fallout of everything, he'd begun to insulate himself. Against his club, his old, loud friends. The women, the music, the booze.

Oh, he still went out. He could not let his reputation suffer completely. But he also spent a lot of time alone and in silence, rewriting the prophecy his father had left for him.

The balcony led to a staircase down to the gardens below, and Luciano met Serena at the top. He held up his palm—an invitation to link hands.

The slight sneer she failed at hiding amused him. So much about her amused him. Perhaps because while she kept that perfect icy mask impeccable in public, when they were alone together she could not seem to help resorting to her true self. Even if that true self hated him, it was amusing.

But she also did what needed doing, and as much as he'd like to hate that about her, he could only respect it.

He felt that she had to respect *something* about him as well to be here. To be doing this. For all her little barbs, she *did* treat him like an equal partner in this. She did not ridicule his ideas. She had not once treated him as his father often had, as if everything he did was the wrong step.

Besides, he had no doubt there was at least some small part of her that *wanted* him. Maybe she didn't like it any better than he did, but it was there. Vibrating underneath the surface. They could both ignore it, they could both use it. It didn't matter. It was *there*. An entity and a being he didn't think either of them knew how to fully parse.

Her hands were soft, fingers long and slender like her legs as they linked with his. For a completely incomprehensible moment, he found himself wondering if so much would be different if they had not been raised as rivals, raised to hate one another. Would there be mutual attraction and respect without all the complicated thorns of being a Valli and an Ascione?

Because if she treated him like an equal, she saw him as one, and that was very rare in his life indeed. He made sure of it.

And why the hell should that matter? It didn't.

There was the faint scent of lavender that seemed to cling to her or the air. He wanted it to be the air, but he'd been in her bed and knew what her sheets smelled of.

He had to fight off a scowl as they descended the staircase. She led him through a pathway through the unlit garden. He only had the general feeling of lots of growth, but the darkness did not give away any detail.

She opened a gate, and out they stepped onto the beach. It was a small slice of sand, mostly barricaded by big rocks. But not too far down the waterline there were lights. Some resorts, along with other houses and estates along the water.

"Do you really think someone would be watching?" Luciano asked.

"What I know is at least two cars followed you up to my gate. My security team will be determining their identity, but I would imagine it was press of some kind. If they know you're here, they know air and sea is the only other way to get a glimpse. I'm not sure we've reached helicopter or drone levels of interest yet."

"*Yet*, being the operative word."

"One hopes. No doubt anyone in Genoa will be intrigued, and the way social media can make a story of anything might give us some global reach, but one never knows what will catch the public's imagination."

"Indeed not."

"So, do I think someone is out there watching?" She gestured out along the shoreline. "I think we have a fifty-fifty chance, so we might as well take it. It's about the only way I'd let your hand hold mine, naturally."

He smiled in spite of himself. "Naturally," he agreed. "But hand holding is so…childish, is it not?" He dropped her hand, lifted his to her back, then slid it down the curve of her spine as they walked. "There are far more intimate touches a man and woman might engage in on a moonlit walk on the beach." He ran his hand back up, curled his fingers around the nape of her neck and felt the shudder there, the soft escape of her breath.

He did not care for how much his own body seemed to shudder in response, but it was all for the end goal. All of it.

"I have some ideas on how to handle the Francos next week," she said after a moment. She did not try to dislodge his hand from her neck. She did not angle herself so that they were not essentially hip to hip as they walked. She even seemed to be trying to relax into his touch, rather than stiffen against it.

But the change of topic was clear. She was accepting the touch on the fifty-fifty chance they were being photographed, but she would not engage in innuendo.

Yet.

So, he responded to her change in topic in kind. "As do I. In fact, I think we should approach this meeting as a team. Go into it together."

"We are not officially a partnership yet," Serena said, a faint frown on her face. "We will need everything in place legally before we start muddying up those waters."

"Then, let us move forward with that."

Starlight dappled the sand. The quiet sounds of waves echoed gently as they walked. If there was any romance in the world, it was in this setting. So, it was time to get on with the show.

He pulled the box from his pocket, fingering the velvet as he watched her.

She looked remote in profile. An untouchable goddess with her hair down and her face upturned to the moon so she seemed to glint silver as she considered his suggestion. For all her strength and determination and *hate* towards him, the moonlight made her seem ethereal. Lit from within. Someone else entirely—like the perfect Serena could be soft and romantic somewhere underneath all those sharp glaciers.

And maybe she could. To someone else. Not to *him*.

The strange pang in his chest at that thought was…nonsensical. Ridiculous.

The tightness in his chest wasn't nerves, because he'd long since vanquished those from his life. It wasn't lust—he knew what that felt like, and while he could not deny the strange appeal Serena had, here in this moment it wasn't a bolt, a sharp need that wound through him.

It was something else altogether. Something he wasn't familiar with. He didn't like it or trust it, so he shoved it away and focused on the plan. He released her neck, stepped back and then dropped to one knee.

And waited for her to turn to him.

CHAPTER EIGHT

SERENA BRACED HERSELF to deal with whatever Luciano had stopped for. Probably a kiss for the cameras. A romantic embrace. It was the smart thing to do, but something about the environment added dread to something she'd already decided.

Because it was romantic—the starlight, the soft lap of waves, the darkness. And when she turned, she would be faced with a far too attractive man, whose simple touch made her shudder and sigh even when she didn't *want* to. When she had worked so hard all her life to make all her reactions just what she wanted them to be.

No matter how hard she tried, she could not make her reactions what she wanted them to be when it came to him. She could not find a safe place in her icy perfection.

She *would* let him touch her. She *would* have to let him kiss her. Perhaps she could continue to protest a *little*, but she needed to start showing a weakening, so she lulled him into complacency.

And she desperately needed to think of it that way, so she did not think about what a kiss might actually feel like. Business over shivers and pulses.

She had already had her lawyers involved in drawing up papers that would solidify their business partnership once they were married. He would no doubt need his lawyers to go over them and counteroffer different things. It was likely to be drawn out, so yes, they should move forward.

But that meant moving forward with the marriage.

She had been so ready to do that, and then they had walked hand in hand, and her body had felt…foreign.

Then he had skimmed his hand along her spine. She understood why cats purred now. How the gentle caress of a hand could make a body feel content and pleasurable. Then he'd put his hand at her neck, and it had been like… little explosions in her bloodstream. No longer just *content*, something more…wanting.

She wanted to focus on business, on what needed to be done, and still her body pulsed even though he'd released her. She squeezed her eyes shut, tried to find some of her always available control.

Upper hand, remember? she told herself. *Not for pleasure…for the upper hand.*

Trying to find a smile, something flirtatious inside of her instead of concern over her body's reactions, she turned to look at him. Except he wasn't standing. He was kneeling in the sand and—

Serena's breath caught. Not at the scene itself—romantic and movie-like as it might be. It was the ring. It glittered there under the celestial lights above, a beacon of pretty… perfection in its cozy little box that Luciano held out to her.

"I considered your style and mine," Luciano said, his voice low and as lulling as the sea waves. "I could have had something designed, but I think we should strike while the iron is hot. It is expensive, indeed, but not quite gaudy as you had indicated you wished for last night. Still, this should do, shouldn't it?"

It was gorgeous. Absolutely, thrillingly beautiful. She was not a flashy person, and the ring bordered on flashy, but not so far that she didn't like it. It was a pink diamond, settled among other winking diamonds on a slim band that made the center stone look that much bigger.

It reminded her of being a child, going through her mother's jewelry boxes. Enjoying the feel of cool precious metals on her fingers and wrists and neck.

But that was a reminder of her mother always telling her that she was too plain for such things. And she was, fair enough. She was plain and unassuming. Dull. This ring didn't match *her*.

But it matched the image of someone who'd caught Luciano Ascione's attention, the fake fiancée for the fake marriage. So she had to go with it. Didn't she?

He gripped her hand and held it still as he slid the ring onto her finger. She wanted to keep her gaze on the ring, but it seemed to move, of its own accord, up to meet his gaze. Dark and intense. Potent, looking up at her. Like a shot of liquor.

Why? She didn't know. Maybe some men were just given that kind of power. So incredibly unfair, but impossible to deny in this moment. She had to lick her lips and swallow in order to speak. "This was a smart move," she managed to say.

He got to his feet and looked down at her, his dark eyes alight with amusement, his mouth curved into something cutting and intriguing at once.

"Why, thank you, *cara*. I so appreciate your approval." His tone was wry. "I suppose that is your way of saying *yes*."

She was afraid to speak. There were too many emotions battering around inside of her, making her throat feel tight. The way her body felt. The way this felt real, when she knew it wasn't, and didn't want it to be. And still, that pulsing *need* throbbing deep inside of her that she had to get a hold of to come out on top. "I suppose it is," she managed.

"Do you think your photographers caught any of that?"

Photographers. The *play* they were essentially acting out. She had to remember that even if the ring was real, even if whatever papers they signed to be married and combine Valli and Ascione were *real*, the whole…personal side of things wasn't.

She wanted to rub at the odd pain in her chest, but couldn't seem to find control of her own body.

"If they don't, I shall be sure to make an appearance somewhere notable with this on my hand. That should start the talk." She frowned down at the ring. "However, I shall have to break the news to my mother first." Something she did not relish. It left a worse taste in her mouth than actually marrying Luciano.

"Ah." His arm came around her, and she could give him credit here—he knew the act. Relished it. She still felt shell-shocked. "Shall I expect pistols at dawn then?" he asked, guiding her back toward her gardens.

Serena shook her head. She felt strangely…afloat. Like she was in a dream where she was a fairy-tale princess, and the handsome man in front of her represented some kind of love and future. She could remember a time when she'd had silly little dreams like that. But she'd been small, naive. It was before she'd realized that she would never achieve that *sparkle* her mother had. Back when her parents had divorced and split their lives forever, shuttling Serena back and forth like an unwanted gift they could not get rid of without offending someone. That was when she realized all she had to offer was perfection, and maybe that would never earn love, but it would get her *somewhere*. It would earn her a place.

She needed to get a hold of herself. It was just a ring. "No, my mother never cared about Valli business. She won't have any compunction on you being an Ascione. She will insist on a dinner and she will…" Serena trailed off. She didn't know exactly how to warn Luciano how her mother would be.

Serena had learned how to be perfect in her father's eyes. How to be what he wanted, more or less. She had been able to work and *prove* to him that she had some worth.

She had never been able to make that kind of dent with her mother. Serena didn't allow that to put them at odds, but she did keep a certain kind of distance from her mother. But a life event like this would require dealing with her, lest she make a scene.

No doubt, Luciano wouldn't even notice. Mother's barbs tended to be for Serena and Serena alone.

But it had to be done. Mother was the only family she had left. And the whole point was everything needed to seem real to outsiders. Her mother would have to be… somewhat involved going forward.

Serena contemplated the sea for a moment. Maybe she could just run into it and swim until she found a deserted island or simply perished instead. But before she could give any serious consideration to running away, Luciano stopped their forward progress toward her home.

"I'm afraid, there is one thing we will have to do before we head back inside and break the happy news to your mother."

"What is that?"

He turned her to face him. When she glanced up at him, she saw that his expression was oddly grave. But then his mouth curved. An attempt at a smile. She thought it might have even been an attempt to be roguishly irritating, but it didn't meet his eyes.

Not as he pulled her body close, so they were pressed together. His heat surrounding them. The smell of the sea, the sounds of the waves, the strange lull of a darkened evening and his hands on her hips. It was like something out of a book or movie. Romantic and…something darker. A strange, twisting need that she might have words for if she wanted to find them.

She didn't.

"We should seal this deal with a kiss, Serena," he said, angling his head down so that his mouth was close to hers. So she could feel his breath along with his body. "Just in case those photographers *are* watching."

She swallowed, trying to think of something smart to say. He was right, of course. This was all an act so they had to act, but…

He did not ask permission. He did not brush his lips across her cheek. He pressed his mouth to hers, pulled her body to his.

And devoured.

* * *

It couldn't be chaste. He'd known that going in. A long lens in the darkness would need a prolonged embrace. They would still likely just be grainy shadows, but a grainy shadow could be used with the right story.

It would need to take its time. It would need…

He lost the thread of his thoughts at the first shudder of her body against his. Something like heat scorched through him. A longing for things he didn't fully recognize and knew better than to try.

So he focused on what he did recognize. The contours of a kiss. The delicate press of her body, surprisingly soft and small. She held herself in such a way, he'd expected something…stronger, he supposed. A leanness with sharp angles ready to cut him to pieces.

He'd also expected her to be more stiff, to push him away, to resist…even if she eventually gave in.

But there was no resistance in her. Innocence maybe, but she allowed his mouth the enticing tour of hers. When he splayed his fingers wide, swept them up her side and settled just short of her breasts, she shuddered out a sigh that had a newly appointed hunger digging its way deep inside of him.

And because it was there—her parted mouth, a mystery too close to walk away from—he tasted. A stunning combination of the wine from dinner and something unique to this kiss and this moment alone.

He supposed her innocence allowed him to set the tone, and there was a delirium in that. He was in charge. Of this moment. Of tough, icy Serena who was none of those things in this moment. She was soft, sweet and a million other words he'd never once used to describe Serena Valli.

Serena Valli.

It was her name that reminded him of who he was and what this was meant to be. He didn't jerk back, though he wanted to. But no, this was an act.

No matter what strange detours his brain, or body, had gone down, this was still just an act. So he carefully eased away. First his mouth, then his body. Until cool air swept between them.

His own body was too hot, too hard. Too prepared for something that had grown more and more tempting as the kiss went on. Oh, he'd planned on seducing her. He'd told himself their chemistry, as it was, might allow him to enjoy it.

Now, he could admit that he was a little concerned it might end in a mistake. Committed by *him*.

Impossible. Unthinkable.

They regarded each other in the short distance they'd created, wary and aroused. A dangerous tightrope. One Luciano realized in a strange way he was as new to as she was. He doubted very much that Serena had ever been buffeted by something as base as physical spontaneous combustion as he had, but he'd never dabbled in *unwanted* desire before. He rarely drew lines like that. If a woman was willing, and they usually were, he slaked whatever desires they both had.

To hold back was new, and he didn't like it. That lust and concern fused with irritation at himself, at their fathers, at the entire damn world for throwing him into a gray area he had never wanted.

"I think that should suffice for tonight," she said coolly. And he might have believed she was cool inside and out, but her hand shook as she reached up to smooth it over her hair.

He wished she were the ice princess he'd once believed her to be. It would be so much easier to set aside that kiss as a one off. But there was something underneath all her veneer, and he'd gotten another intriguing peek at it.

Damn her.

"Indeed," he managed to grit out.

"And you will take the window seat tonight," she said firmly, an order, then marched into the gardens, leaving him behind in the dark.

Hard and aching for a woman he wanted nothing to do with.

CHAPTER NINE

SERENA FOUND THAT having her own bed back had done nothing to help her sleep, with Luciano stretched out on her window seat. She had tossed and turned and…throbbed and ached for half the night.

She hated to think what she might have done with herself if she'd been alone. The thought *haunted* her, no matter how she tried to set it away. She had not known that pretending could be…

Well, it didn't matter what it could be. What mattered was how she was going to deal with it. In reality, it was a *good thing*, part of the plan. He'd kissed her for the cameras, and ideally, she'd fooled him enough that he'd gone to sleep thinking she'd enjoyed it.

You did enjoy it.

And that was the disturbing fact she kept coming back to. She had wanted more. Giving into any kind of seduction last night would not have been part of any *plan*.

Not that he'd tried to seduce her. He'd eased away from that kiss, stepped away from her as if he'd…tasted something bad. But for a while, for the majority of that kiss, he had not.

She had nothing to compare it to, but it had *seemed* like he'd had a physical reaction somewhat on par with hers.

An act. Of course it was an act. Everything they did except hate each other was an act. And the act was important. Which was why she slipped out of bed, shrugged on her robe and grabbed her phone. She had an order of business to get over with.

She stepped quietly out of the room and took the door out onto the balcony that overlooked the sea, the colorful buildings crowded along the shoreline. And her, alone and isolated on her castle on the hill.

Just where she wanted to be. What she did not want was to do what must be done, but she could hardly put it off if pictures of last night started to circulate. She took in steadying breaths of air, let it wash through her and fill her with calm.

She would need it.

She dialed her mother's number, watched the morning sunlight dapple across the water. Part of her hoped her mother wouldn't answer, and she couldn't help feeling ashamed of that hope. Even if her mother didn't deserve her devotion, she was not an *evil* woman. Just a self-centered one, who didn't realize how words could hurt.

"Serena." The greeting was tinged with disappointment. "Haven't we discussed how busy I am in the mornings and how little I like to have conversations before lunchtime?"

Serena didn't sigh. "I apologize, Mother."

Angelica Valli—she'd kept her ex-husband's last name despite many romantic partners since because she liked the cache it gave her and the opportunity to discuss what a terrible husband he'd been—sighed heavily.

In her youth, she'd been an actress, and she still missed the stage so played whatever role she could whenever life gave her the opportunity. She liked attention in whatever ways she could get it, and she was very good at getting it.

The one role she'd never played well, from Serena's point of view, was mother.

But that was neither here nor there.

"I have some news, and as it will likely be made public soon, I wanted to tell you first," Serena said, being careful to keep her voice neutral. "It won't require any conversation at all. I am engaged. To be married." She stared at the beautiful ring on her finger. If nothing else, her mother would certainly be impressed with that.

Her mother laughed, and Serena winced in spite of herself. The caustic sound reminded her too much of how uncomfortable she'd been in her mother's care. Neither of her parents had quite known what to do with her, and as much as her father had not been a loving or devoted man, he'd mostly ignored her.

Angelica preferred to *poke*. It had been there before the divorce but had only gotten worse after.

You'll always be as dull and uninspiring as your father. Nothing I could do could change it.

Yes, Angelica had always made it clear there was nothing to be done, so Serena had leaned into the *dull*—which was where she felt most comfortable. And in the dull, in the *as your father*, she had found her mark.

She had made herself into a businesswoman to *rival* her father. So perfect, so smart, so cunning that even he who had no interest in her at all had been forced to admit she was an asset to Valli.

"Well, that *is* interesting," Angelica said after a while. "I hope you'll be smart enough to protect your own assets, while getting access to as many of his as possible. Don't let romantic notions fool you."

"Of course not."

No congratulations. Not even excitement over the prospect of a wedding. Just: *make sure to protect your assets*.

Which was fine, because this was entirely about her assets, even if her mother didn't know that.

"Is that all?" Mother asked. No questions about a wedding, or even about the man in question. Just *is that all*. Serena did not understand why she thought there might be more, except her mother had always told her to focus on tricking a man into marrying her, rather than do something so boring as go into the Valli *business*.

And here she was, doing both. And Mother didn't care. *Why did you think she would?*

Serena had to clear her throat to speak. To finish the conversation with all the pertinent information, no matter how much she preferred to just hang up. "I believe you know of my fiancée." As if mentioning him conjured him, Luciano stepped out onto the balcony wearing black trousers and a button-down shirt.

Unbuttoned. With sleep-tousled hair. And still too unfairly beautiful in spite of it. He looked like an ad for cologne or expensive watches.

"I cannot imagine I'd know anyone who would find themselves engaged to you, darling. We move in *much* different circles socially."

Socially, maybe, but the men she did business with tended to be in the monetary echelon that her mother preferred to socialize with. She did not know if Mother and Luciano had ever been properly introduced, but no doubt Mother had been to his club. No doubt Mother knew just who he was and what his financial portfolio looked like.

Something about that made her hesitate, but any hesitation about giving her mother this information and dreading what she'd do about it had to be moved past. This needed to be done. "Luciano Ascione."

He did a little mock bow, as if she'd introduced him to a crowd of people who were thrilled and applauding. It had a foreign feeling settling in her chest. Almost like amusement, when a conversation with her mother never had any of that.

There was a beat of silence, and Serena would blame Luciano distracting her on the fact that she was not prepared and braced for her mother's reaction.

"Serena. You cannot be this stupid."

Serena blinked, stiffened even though she'd taught herself long ago not to let her mother's barbs land. "I beg your pardon?"

"What would a man like Luciano Ascione want with *you*?"

The question was an honest one, even if it twisted in Serena like old insecurities she'd forced herself to leave behind. Mother didn't *mean* anything by it. She simply and honestly did not understand.

And Serena knew she'd never be able to convince her mother, but she supposed she had to at least pretend to try. "I'm sure it does not seem like it on paper, but Luciano and I actually have quite a bit in common."

Luciano raised an eyebrow, and the strangest sensation

of wanting to laugh overtook the dull ache of dealing with her mother. Perhaps she should always have him around when handling this kind of undertaking.

Luciano held out his hand, a kind of sign that he wanted the phone.

She nearly did laugh out loud then. She shook her head, tried to remember what she'd been about to tell her mother. They had things in common and…

He made the gesture again. Serena turned away from him so he couldn't distract her anymore. "Mother—"

The phone was plucked from her fingers and she whirled around to try to retrieve it, but Luciano held her phone to his ear and his arm out like he was warding her off.

"Mrs. Valli, so good to talk to you," he greeted cheerfully. "Luciano Ascione here. I'm not sure we've ever spoken, but of course Serena has told me much about you, and I believe you were friendly with my uncle for a time."

Serena advanced on him, trying to reach for the phone, but his free hand clasped her wrist and held her out of reach. An easy display of his height and strength.

"Serena accepted my proposal just last night. I like to believe I've won over her suspicious nature, but I won't be able to believe it for sure until she introduces me to you."

Serena considered kicking him in the shin, but she must have telegraphed the thought because he quickly dropped her hand and took two steps away. Humor danced in his eyes while she hoped murder danced in hers.

She tried to advance again, quickly this time. A quick grab out and she'd have the phone and—

Instead, she found her back plastered to his chest, one muscular arm of his banded around her midsection, holding her arms down at their sides. Effectively immobilizing her. She was so shocked that for a moment, she only stood there, fully still. Fully…something.

If anyone came upon them, it would look a bit like a lover's embrace with his chin tucked over the top of her head. Rage warred with the unfamiliar feeling of being so close to someone, held so tight. It wasn't *threatening*. She didn't feel the desperate need to escape.

No, she felt…held. And the foreign feeling of wanting to sink into something so…strong. So warm. A direct antithesis to the morning.

But it was annoying, she reminded herself. He should not be talking to her mother. He should not be…any of this.

She lifted one leg, trying to determine if she could bend it at the right angle to come into hard, painful contact with a vulnerable part of his body.

He chuckled and the rumble of his chest against her back reminded her, so unfortunately, of last night. Of the way it had rippled through her when she'd felt his heart thud against hers, body to body, mouth to mouth. So that security meshed with that unfamiliar *pulse*, and she didn't know what to make of any of it.

"We would like to invite you to dinner," Luciano was saying in a voice full of cheerful vivacity. "If your schedule would allow it, of course. To celebrate our most happy news."

Oh…no, was all Serena could think and she began to squirm in earnest. She had to stop this. Luciano's grip was tight, but she could move the lower half of her body. If she twisted back and forth…

"I'll work out the details and send a formal invitation once it is set. Let me give you back to Serena."

So quickly that she nearly stumbled forward, he released her. He held out the phone to her, his mouth curved into an amused smile. But there was something about the look in his eye, the way he'd angled the lower half of his body away from her that left her feeling suddenly...winded. Like they had narrowly missed...something.

But she could hear her mother's voice coming from the receiver and had to lift the phone to her ear.

"I suppose I will come to dinner," Mother was saying, sounding so affronted and exhausted by such a simple request. "But I can't promise I will be able to pretend this is anything but an embarrassment."

"Mother, you don't have—"

But before she could finish, Mother was saying good-bye and hanging up.

Serena whirled on Luciano. She felt too many things to parse, and she knew better than to let loose with temper when she was churned up in ways she didn't understand. But she hated him.

Hated.

"You shouldn't have done that."

"Why not?" he returned in that maddeningly insouciant way of his. "She will have to be at the wedding. Besides, if we have the dinner somewhere public, there's another opportunity to be seen. If I am not mistaken, your mother loves to be seen."

"Yes, she does. In any way she can. She also enjoys to *cause* a scene, and since she thinks this is an *embarrass-*

ment and I am stupid for thinking you could want to marry me, this can only end in disaster."

For a moment, Luciano said nothing. He studied her with a kind of seriousness she did not recall ever seeing in him before. It made her…nervous. Like he could…understand all the twisted pieces inside of her that Mother managed to work up no matter how hard Serena tried to remain unmoved.

She knew very little about his upbringing, except that Gianluca Ascione had been a hard and exacting man to everyone in his life—including his son.

This realization poked holes in her growing balloon of rage and had her deflating into something…tired. She just felt *exhausted*. Like no matter how hard she tried, all her perfection was an impossible wall to keep building, because *he* would always slip through the cracks.

"Then we shall have a dinner at my penthouse," he finally said.

It would be easier. Mother hated the castle. But… "Why?"

Luciano shrugged. "If she is going to make a scene, I prefer handling scenes on my home battlefield." His smile was sharp. "Besides, it gives us an opportunity to have people see you and your mother go into my building, without anyone seeing the scene itself. This is our goal, is it not?"

She closed her eyes, pinched the bridge of her nose and turned away from him and toward the balcony. She rested her elbows on the rail and took a deep breath of sea air in.

She felt him come behind her and she tensed, for too many reasons, really. But somehow she knew he would touch her. She thought she didn't want him to. She wanted it to be because she didn't want to be touched by *him*, but she did. And that's what she didn't want. This constant proof that she wanted more of his hands on her, and all her denials were just that. *Denial*.

Then he pushed his thumb against the tight muscle in her neck, and she could be embarrassed later at the happy sigh that escaped her mouth. *God* that felt good.

"Did you not sleep well, *cara*?" he asked in a soft, sultry murmur.

She was tempted to melt into the touch, into the quiet lull of his voice. His thumb rubbed circles against her neck and it was truly a glorious relaxation. It hit the exact right spot that had tensed and tensed and tensed. She wanted him to do that forever.

Until she remembered she hated him. And the fact his question was just him being a jerk, not actually expressing concern.

"I slept beautifully," she replied, stepping away from his hands. They were a problem. And while she was planning on giving in to the seduction route, sometimes, a girl had to know when to retreat. "And now, I need to get to work."

"*We*, darling," he said, holding out his elbow like he expected her to loop her arm with his. "We will head into work together this morning."

Serena had not fought him as much as he'd anticipated. She'd surveyed him with that regal disdain as he'd explained that they should take turns going into each other's offices, begin to lay the groundwork for a merger while the lawyers drew up contracts and what not.

And show off her ring. The stories should start weaving their way through their mutual acquaintances, so giving everyone something even more concrete to talk about would be good. He had no doubt that both he and Serena would have all sorts of meetings lined up—customers who had left crawling back and begging for a moment just to get a sniff of gossip.

Then, together, they would offer a new deal that the Americans would not be able to match. Serena's home-grown connections. Luciano's ironclad global partnerships. Together, they would offer their customers *everything*.

It was such a good plan, he sometimes forgot it was hers.

They walked into the Valli office building, arm in arm yet again. Serena ensured it was her left hand in his, so the diamond was what anyone would come face to face with as they approached.

She greeted anyone they came across by name—something the Vallis were famous for. A personal approach. Family to family. Ironic considering how little of a family man Serena's father had been, but in the confines of these walls, Mr. Valli had built his own family. And made a lot of money from it.

His own father had considered it beneath him. He'd gone for the glitz, the glamour. A royal kind of viewpoint, handed down from generation to generation. A counterpoint to the allegedly humble Vallis—which of course had only infuriated his father, because they'd amassed as big a fortune as he had.

Honestly, both methods were just smoke and mirrors to hide the fact that both men were ill-equipped to manage the legacies handed down to them.

Ironic that their children should seek to save said legacies. Together.

When they stepped out of the elevator on a higher floor, Luciano realized that this would be *her* floor. The woman behind a desk that guarded the hallway of doors immediately jumped to her feet.

"Good morning, Andrea," Serena greeted, moving in a straight shot toward whatever target she sought. But as she passed the desk of who Luciano assumed was Serena's assistant, Serena paused and turned to look at this Andrea.

Luciano watched as Serena carefully composed herself, put on that fake smile she was so good at. Meanwhile, the assistant couldn't seem to stop herself from staring, openmouthed, at the diamond on Serena's hand.

"Andrea, I'd like to introduce you to my fiancée, Mr. Luciano Ascione. You will likely be seeing quite a bit of him in the coming months. I hope I can count on you to help him feel welcome and at home here at Valli."

"O-of course. Welcome, Mr. Ascione." The woman hesitated, like she wasn't quite sure how to greet him. A handshake. A curtsy. A spitted oath.

"Thank you, Andrea." He offered her a warm smile, trying to balance his usual charm with something more… homey. He did not think he succeeded when Andrea's cheeks turned a faint shade of pink.

"We will be in my office. You can send any phone calls through, but please no visitors."

"Yes, ma'am. Ms. Valli—"

But before she could say whatever she was going to say, a group of men appeared in the hallway it appeared Serena had been meaning to go down. Luciano didn't think *they* noticed the change in Serena's demeanor. It was very subtle.

But clearly a kind of putting on armor.

"Serena," one of the men said. He had a thick mustache and heavy middle. Luciano thought he recognized him as one of the Valli high-level managers his father had once tried to woo away from Valli.

"We've called an emergency meeting," the man said firmly. Like a father might tell a child they were grounded.

Every single man blocking their way stared at Luciano with disapproving eyes. Honestly, it wasn't all that different than being in his own office. Disapproval was comfortable and easy. Especially in these circumstances, he liked that they felt like a challenge.

"You'll need to discuss an appropriate time in my schedule with Andrea," Serena replied dismissively.

"We already have."

Serena looked back at Andrea, who nodded nervously. "You had space at ten-thirty and they were very...determined."

"Very well. I will see you then. If you'll excuse us." She gave them an imperious glare, gestured for them to move out of her way.

With her left hand. Luciano watched as every single one of them zeroed their gaze to the ring on it. There was not surprise, but there was consternation. But they shuffled out of the way so Serena could march through.

She led Luciano to what he assumed was the door of her office. She opened it and gestured him inside.

"Serena, this is very perplexing," one of the men said, making a move as if he'd follow her into her office.

"For you," she said cheerfully. Then she shut the door on his face, without so much of a hint of regret. She moved to her desk and placed her briefcase on it. Every move was precise and economical, as if she didn't care one bit about the grumpy old men in the hall.

"Did your father really trust those dimwits?" Luciano asked casually, wondering if she'd leap to their defense when it came to him.

She did not. "I am afraid so. They agreed with whatever he said, and that is how my father preferred to run a business."

"But not you?"

"Why would I surround myself with people who agree with me when I could surround myself with intelligence and tact and ensure that I have the best operations by nature of the fact I'm bringing sharp minds together for a common goal?" She moved about her desk with impatient movements—a woman on a mission.

It surprised him a little to hear her say this. She seemed so determined and sure of herself, he was surprised she gave any time to anyone else's intelligence or sharp mind. Also, it sounded too close to how he managed his business. "I quite agree with you," he said, settling himself into a cushy armchair in the corner.

The office itself was sparse, minimalist and not at all like her or her home. But this chair was cozy and comfortable, and no doubt something she'd chosen for herself.

"Yes," she surprised him by saying, instead of trying to eviscerate him with some politely delivered stab at his intelligence, or lack thereof. "I looked into your club."

He watched her face, especially when she expressly did

not meet his gaze. "Did you?" he murmured, intrigued that she might look into anything that had to do with him. But maybe he shouldn't have, and maybe he shouldn't be pleased. If she'd looked into it, it was no doubt to get her hands on it later.

He'd blow it up himself first.

"I expected, like so many trust fund babies, you would have filled the books with paying off school cronies and others riding the coattails of their family's wealth," she said, settling down to her laptop. "Instead, you've hired some heavy hitters."

"Your acting is improving. You don't even sound shocked."

"I wouldn't say your ability to make a decent business decision *shocks* me," she said thoughtfully. "Not at this point. You are not quite as dim as I would have liked to have given you credit for."

"Why, Serena, I must be rubbing off on you. Has our kiss or my ring robbed you of your senses?"

Then she did meet his gaze. She even smiled. "It must be both."

It was a joke, bordering on flirtatious, and Luciano could not account for the way that made his chest tight. Made him think of said kiss, of her body pressed to his—on the beach last night, on the balcony this morning. How different and intriguing she was. How completely, uniquely *her*.

He did not know anyone like her. Except, just maybe, himself. Though he did not share her strange obsession with animals and floral.

Their gazes held a few beats too long, just like at the beach last night. When she finally looked away, he'd hoped it'd feel like he won a challenge.

It didn't. It felt like a loss.

"You'll attend the meeting with me. We'll outline our plan—the parts they need to know anyway. Then we'll meet with the lawyers. We'll need to move that along so no one can attempt to throw a wrench in it."

"Which means we'll also need to move the wedding along, don't you think?"

She sighed, but she didn't argue with him. "Yes. The sooner the better."

CHAPTER TEN

SERENA LED LUCIANO to the meeting room. She didn't feel nervous. Even if Luciano was his obnoxious self, she knew how to handle these men.

And, at the end of the day, they had no power over her. They'd try to find some. They'd try to stop her. But they hadn't been able to yet. And, much as she hated to admit it, in a war like this, Luciano would no doubt be an asset. She tended to focus too much on the *should be* and not enough on the underhanded ways people could behave when their power was threatened.

She hadn't threatened this group's power, except by the fact she was a woman and younger. She couldn't help but wonder how different this would all be if she'd been her father's only *son*.

But that was neither here nor there.

She could fire them all, but she knew that would lead to revenge plots. That too she could handle, but she didn't want to. Not yet. So she kept them on. Pretended to listen to their manly tutting. Then did however she pleased.

"Serena." Riccardo Esposito was her least favorite of this group. He always talked to her as if she was perennially twelve. The only reason she hadn't fired him was because she was afraid the other three would get so worked up about it, they'd cause problems she couldn't yet afford.

Someday. Someday, they'd all be gone in one fell swoop. But for today, she had to deal with them as she always had. Endlessly polite. Carefully cool. Unbothered by their complaints and criticisms.

And sure of what she was doing.

"This is a business meeting," Riccardo said, as if this was news.

Serena settled herself at the head of the meeting table, and Luciano gracefully slid into the seat Riccardo had no doubt been about to sit in. Serena had to bite the inside of her cheek to keep from laughing at the mottled red of Riccardo's cheeks.

"It *is* a business meeting. On company time and everything," Serena agreed as the rest of the men took seats. "So, let's move this along."

"*He* is not part of our business."

"I'm afraid that won't be the case for much longer." Serena smiled placidly. "The lawyers are already working on a Valli-Ascione merger. We're still working out the details, but all your jobs will be safe, of course."

"For a period of time anyway," Luciano murmured.

Serena supposed she should have found his input irritating, but it hit just the right note. A bad cop, good cop kind of approach.

She met disdainful and disapproving gazes of the four men who'd been her father's top advisors. Serena had let them maintain their positions, and she listened to their suggestions still, out of respect for what they'd done for Valli previously.

But she rarely listened to their outdated and insipid ideas. Her father had hired and trusted *yes men*, not brilliant minds.

Since Riccardo had never found a seat, he stood there vibrating. "A merger would violate everything your father stood for."

"My father apparently valued drinking, driving and killing himself. So, this is not quite the censure I think it was meant to be."

"Your grandfather—"

"You did not work for my grandfather," Serena cut off coolly. She did not let the simmering anger that they would *dare* mention her grandfather to her permeate her tone or her expression. "You did not know my grandfather. You will not invoke his name if you wish to remain employed, and let me take it a step further." She met Riccardo's furious gaze, cool as a cucumber. "I am in control. Full control. If Valli fails, that will be on my shoulders. Not yours. So I will make the decisions. And this decision? It saves us."

"Serena." It was Mattia Adamo's turn to try to reason with her. She could tell from the way he said her name. "This is a huge decision and an incredibly large undertaking. You cannot expect us to approve simply because you…" His gaze slid to Luciano. Disdain hardened his gaze. "Because you have found yourself personally involved with our *rival*." His gaze returned to her, a paternal and patronizing smile on his face. "You must give this time."

All generous understanding, with the undercurrent of condescension that was close enough to remind her of her mother's disapproval.

Funny, that never bothered her here. It never had. Her

mother still had a knack for twisting a knife Serena fully didn't understand, but these men were…nothing to her. They were forever simply obstacles in her way, and she appreciated that role for them. You could not stay sharp if you were not continually tested.

But if they got too far into her way now, they would have to be cut. And she would deal with the fallout, even if she didn't want to just yet.

"My dear boys," Luciano said, and the way he drawled out the word *boys* set every single man in this room's teeth on edge.

Serena relished it.

"*Rival* is such an antiquated word in this current landscape." Luciano gave every impression of the relaxed, borderline bored, playboy. But his words were absolutely true. "The American company has swooped in and hurt us both. Because they can offer *both* global and local services. Because they can throw a few minnows our way and have us fighting for the scraps of it all like starving sharks. Let us not be desperate. Let us be smart."

"And merging companies would be smart because…?" Riccardo asked this with malice, and yet, Serena could not help but note he waited for an answer. He might *hate* Luciano, but he did not try to treat him like a child speaking out of turn.

"I'm sure once Serena shares her plan company-wide you'll have all the answers you need." He gestured at her, and she had to hold herself carefully still lest she give away her surprise.

All of this was an act, but she hadn't counted on him to act like anything was all *her* plan, or particularly smart.

"Now, is that all, gentlemen?" Serena asked, making a production out of standing. "I have an afternoon full of meetings. The work of wooing customers back my father lost from his own stubborn refusal to move on with the times awaits. For all of us," she added pointedly.

"You cannot announce an engagement, a merger, as though you are a dictator," Riccardo said, overloud and as close to losing his temper in a business meeting as Serena had ever seen.

"Mr. Esposito, please. Calm down." Luciano clucked his tongue and glanced at Serena. "Surely Valli employees are reprimanded in some way if they should throw a little tantrum?" He phrased it like a question.

The splutter that came from all four men was truly a thing of beauty. Serena might have clapped if it wouldn't ruin her illusion of cool, controlled leader. "I think that will be all for now, gentlemen. Should you want to discuss this more…calmly…after you've read through my plan, which will be sent out once the lawyers are satisfied, we can call another meeting." She began to move for the door.

Luciano stepped outside the meeting room first, but Riccardo all but leaped in front of the door before Serena could follow.

"You can't do this."

"On that, you are wrong. If you recall, that is exactly how my father set up his version of Valli. One fully in control leader. No checks. No balances. No *cannots*. I hope to change that eventually, but for now, all decision making goes through me and only me. Now, if you'll excuse me."

She pushed past him, only to be stopped by Vincenzo

Conte. "Serena. Please, reconsider. You know that I'm only looking out for you."

She had thought that in the beginning. Of the four of them, she had considered Vincenzo something of a mentor. But in the aftermath of her father's death, she had quickly realized that just because he didn't argue with her, it didn't mean he *supported* her. He was more chameleon than businessman. Out to maintain and amass more power, not save Valli.

She did not trust him, but she pretended. So she smiled. "I appreciate the concern, but I have given this as much thought as anything. It is the right pathway forward."

Vincenzo sighed, clearly meaning to convey concerned disapproval. "What could you possibly see in that man?" he asked her gently.

She looked at Luciano, standing there in the hallway, an amused, satisfied smile on his face. He'd handled the room beautifully. He had a goal, much like she did. They would become enemies again, no doubt, but right now...?

Right now, they were on the same team. And she did see something in him. Something she didn't particularly care to.

"A kindred spirit," she muttered, detesting the fact that it wasn't altogether untrue.

They went through the next few days like this. He went to Valli. She went to Ascione. They met with lawyers. They drew up papers. They planned a wedding.

Serena suggested they could stand a few days not staying in the same place since the papers were abuzz with engagement news, and since that wasn't completely wrong, Luciano had agreed.

Taking space here and there would be essential in keeping his guard up. And it allowed him to think, to plan, to reassess.

Most importantly, he was collecting pieces of her soft spots. By watching her every day. In her own territory. In his. And so he began to notice the things that didn't just irritate her—him, mostly—but the things that offended her. A use of her grandfather's name against her. Anyone at Valli telling her she *couldn't*. Her easy camaraderie with animals and the way she required concentration to appear easy with people.

The way she appeared at ease and peaceful every day in Ascione, but he could see her gaze taking in everything. Without fail, she went home every night, went through the elaborate process of getting one of her notebooks and fancy pens out and then wrote every last thing down.

Meticulous. Determined. Controlled. A fascinating woman, all in all. He could not say he'd ever known someone quite like her. Underneath all that ice was something far more complicated. And a little odd, truly.

But there *were* those soft spots. All of them noted— mentally because he did not require *notebooks*—to be used later when they would suit him, help him. When *he* would have to come out on top.

He told himself this, because it was a much more palatable reason for his interest. Self-preservation over…

Over being fascinated by her.

He scowled a bit because as good as he was at denial, he was having a hard time believing his own lies when it came to *her*.

The *her* who swept into his penthouse early in the af-

ternoon wearing a cheerful summer dress that he wouldn't
have thought suited her at all. She carried a large bouquet
of flowers tucked into one arm and a large bag hanging
off the other.

But she stopped short, because he was no fool. Flowers had already been taken care of, and the caterer was
hard at work in the kitchen, filling the penthouse with delicious smells.

"Oh," was all she said by way of greeting, frowning
at the colorful floral centerpieces that had been delivered
that morning.

"What's in the bag?" he asked, curious what else she
thought he wouldn't have planned for.

"Simply some of my things. It's been a few nights, so I
thought it best if I spend the night here tonight. We haven't
done that yet."

"No, we have not." Fascinating that she'd be the one to
instigate it. "I seem to recall something about gunpoint
needing to be involved if that were to happen?"

She got very prim looking, that haughty chin of hers
going up. "I was referring to your estate when I said that.
An apartment in the city is little different than a hotel, all
things considered."

It was semantics, of course, but he could admit he appreciated her ability to twist semantics to suit herself.

She moved forward, shoved the bag at him. "If you have
an extra room, put this in there. If not, we'll deal with it
after dinner, but you should put it away. I shall see about
adding these flowers to the bouquet."

She was a woman so used to giving orders and expect-
ing them to be followed, that there seemed to be no ques-

tion in her mind whether he'd follow through. He, however, was not a man used to taking orders, so while he took the shoved bag, he did not immediately move to *stow it away*.

She, however, moved for the table—already elaborately set—and unwrapped the flowers. She didn't even *look* at him as she fussed with the centerpiece.

Though she hid it well, he could read the nerves under the surface. He was learning to see under that careful, icy facade. He wanted to believe that was just good business sense, but he knew part of it was pure fascination.

He didn't *revel* in understanding her, but he couldn't seem to stop himself from trying to.

Her mother was coming over for dinner tonight, and if there was one soft spot he still didn't fully understand it was the one that involved her mother. He aimed to figure it out tonight.

So, with that thought in mind, he decided to fully embrace his acted role of doting fiancée. He went and stowed her bag in his bedroom, then returned to the dining room that featured a curved wall of floor-to-ceiling windows to show off the beautiful cityscape and the sea.

He realized, somewhat abruptly, that there at the edge of the far window, if he angled himself just so, he could just make out the jut of rock her little castle settled itself upon.

He wished he had not realized this. It felt strangely…intimate to know he could look out, look across, and see the place he knew represented her true self better than anything she ever let people see.

"It's a beautiful view," Serena said, without ever looking up from her flowers. She was just about done with them, but she took her time with the last stems and arranging them into the centerpiece that already existed.

Luciano made a noncommittal noise as Serena finished what she was doing. He had never once felt uncomfortable in his own home, but suddenly he didn't know quite what to do with himself.

It felt dangerous to think of her *true self* when her mother would not be here for some time yet. When it was just the two of them. Waiting.

"Perhaps I should give you a tour, so it appears to your mother as if you've been here before."

"Good idea," she agreed, but did not immediately move away from the centerpiece.

Luciano tried to find something to say that might irritate her, get that stiff back and cool look of hers geared toward him. But he couldn't seem to think of anything.

Maybe he was ill.

Eventually she let the flowers be and moved closer to where he stood in the living room. She straightened her shoulders, much like she'd done before going into that meeting with her coworkers the other day.

He half expected some dressing down.

"Before we begin, I feel it necessary to explain that… Well, it's just that my mother will be…" She trailed off. The nerves never showed on her face. They were in the way she gripped her hands together, then seemed to realize it and dropped her hands at her sides. She had done this at least five times since arriving. "I do not know how to articulate how my mother will be, but it will not be comfortable or…normal."

He found her nerves strange, but he didn't like it.

"Luckily I am an Ascione. Well versed in uncomfortable and abnormal."

Her mouth curved at that, and a strange warmth settled in his chest. Because it was a real smile. He'd amused her, settled some of those nerves.

And he liked being able to do so.

He could not for the life of him fathom what that *meant*, so he pushed it away as he pushed away so many confusing things when it came to her.

He showed her around the rest of the place feeling a new sort of tension creep into him. It reminded him of a time long gone that he'd gone through great efforts to ignore. That part of his youth when he'd still endeavored to impress his father.

The idea he wanted to impress *her* was a personal affront, and he rejected it. He had to reject it.

Luckily the announcement of Serena's mother's arrival interrupted his thoughts on the matter, and he lead Serena to her mother, plastering on a broad smile fit for the host of the evening.

At first glance, Serena didn't look anything like her mother. The woman was blonde, perhaps a little too thin, but knew how to perfectly accentuate her assets. A beautiful woman. The kind Luciano tended to gravitate toward. There was a sharpness to her that was the complete opposite of Serena's sharpness.

Mrs. Valli clearly knew how to move around the world as an important businessman's ex-wife. She knew how to dress and flatter and what parties to go to in order to be seen. She had the *socialite* part of her role down while Serena channeled all her energy into understanding the business. As long as she had that crutch, she did very well for herself. But left to her own devices, well, she'd no doubt be home with her cats.

No, he could not see any similarities between the two women, and when Serena did not immediately step in as she often did, Luciano knew it would be his role to take the lead tonight. Between two opposing, though related, forces.

Luciano moved forward, all gallantry. "Welcome to my home, Mrs. Valli. I hope you'll allow Eduardo here to take your things."

She gave a little nod and handed off her wrap and purse. "May we get you a drink?"

Mrs. Valli studied the butler, Luciano and the room around them with quick, cunning eyes. "Surprise me."

The butler nodded his head and then disappeared. Before Luciano could guide Serena's mother deeper into the apartment, she reached out and grabbed Serena's left hand. She drew the engagement ring into the light, moved Serena's hand this way and then that. Luciano could not account for how *stiff* Serena seemed as her mother studied the ring on her finger.

"It's positively exquisite," Mrs. Valli said, with very little inflection. Then she trilled out a little laugh as she finally dropped Serena's hand. "Honestly, it looks more suited to me than it could ever be to you, darling."

"I quite like it," Serena said, and Luciano could not ignore the note of hurt in her voice that she tried to hide.

"Of course you do," Mrs. Valli tutted. "It's *gorgeous*. It's simply that a gorgeous piece like this tends to require a…" The woman sighed and pouted a little as she studied her daughter. Then her gaze turned to Luciano. "You know what I mean."

He did not, but as his goal was to charm Serena's mother, he smiled broadly and gestured her inside. "Come. Sit. Let us drink to a happy future together."

Mrs. Valli made a noncommittal noise, but she stepped ahead with Serena toward the dining room and the well-appointed table just as the waitstaff appeared with the drinks and the *primi*.

"You have a quaint little place here," Mrs. Valli said as Luciano held out a chair for her. She seated herself grandly while Luciano tried to deal with the strange slight of his expensive and luxurious penthouse being called *quaint* and *little*.

"Grazie," Luciano managed to mutter before moving to the next seat and holding it out for Serena. "I thought having a nice, private celebration of our families joining would allow us a better opportunity to get to know one another."

Mrs. Valli made that same odd humming sound, that was somehow both polite and a disagreement at the same time. Luciano looked at Serena. Her gaze was out the windows, as though, inside her mind, she was anywhere but here.

Luciano found he hated that too. Because he had never once seen Serena remove herself like this. She was always the first to handle things, putting on that armor and brave face to handle whatever needed to be dealt with.

What would cause her to shrink in on herself instead? His gaze turned to the mother, and he wondered if his *charm* tactics were all wrong. He took his own seat at the head of the table and lifted his glass. "A toast?"

Serena blinked, as if awoken from some spell, but then

held up her glass as well. Mrs. Valli, however, only looked from the glass set in front of her, to the ring on Serena's hand, to him. Her lips were pressed together as if in deep thought. Then, after a great drawn-out moment, she raised her glass and smiled.

"Let me congratulate you both. It's an inspired decision, truly."

Luciano thought the choice of words odd, but there was no point dwelling on it. *"Salute."*

Serena echoed the word with little inflection. There was no fierce determination. No ice. No fire. She seemed a ghost in her own skin.

As they ate, Luciano shared the details of the wedding planning he and Serena had agreed upon. If he managed to lure her into conversation, she gave one-word responses. Everything about her was muted, dull.

Mrs. Valli, on the other hand, was vibrant and talkative. And *vocal* about what she approved of. What she didn't. In some ways, he could see Serena in the woman. The way she noticed everything, filed it away.

But there was an *unnecessary* cruelty to her that Serena didn't have. When they'd discussed the procession and forgoing the tradition of having someone walk Serena down the aisle, Mrs. Valli had rolled her eyes.

"I'm surprised there's no animal parade walking her down the aisle."

"What a lovely idea, Mother," was the only thing Serena said the whole dinner that reminded Luciano of the *actual* Serena.

She was clearly being sarcastic, but Mrs. Valli used it as an opportunity to complain about Serena's cats and the crumbling castle she haunted, and then reached over to touch Serena's styled hair. "How many times have I told you to leave it loose? You look like an ill Victorian child with it all scraped back from your face."

"Perhaps it was the look I was going for."

"*I* quite like it," Luciano added. "For whatever that says about me." He chuckled genially.

Mrs. Valli did not join in, but Serena *almost* smiled.

By the time they got to dessert, Luciano got the impression that Mrs. Valli had drank more than her fill. She spoke a bit overloud and enthusiastically, which only seemed to make Serena shrink in on herself even more. That hint of her old self was a fleeting thing he wished he could find a way to tease out again.

Mrs. Valli let out a loud sigh that had Serena flinching—her first outward reaction since the beginning of the evening.

"Let us drop these niceties," she said, leaning forward so that she met his gaze. "I know you are no doubt a skilled actor, Luciano, but do you really think you can get the public to believe you're interested in Serena?"

For a moment, the words didn't fully penetrate. They were so different than anything he'd expected to hear that he did not know how to absorb her meaning. "I beg your pardon."

"It seems very obvious this is some sort of business ploy. And while I commend you for having that kind of…spirit about you, you don't honestly think people will fall for it? Aside from Serena, of course."

There were so many insults in those few words, Luciano could scarcely understand them all. Especially with Serena sitting right *there* and not offering any kind of fiery or icy rebuttal like she would have if he'd said these things.

But she did not say anything. She was nothing but blood-less ice. No, not even ice. Just…dull, gray rock.

He, on the other hand, felt like all the blood had rushed to his head. In anger and outrage. Some of it misplaced, he knew. Some of Mrs. Valli's behavior felt far too familiar. It was just usually aimed at him, not someone else.

Still, this was about Serena. And her mother. So he cleared his throat and attempted to speak carefully. Not letting his own issues bleed into this. "Mrs. Valli, I think it is very obvious to *me*, you misunderstand much. There is no…trick I'm trying to pull over on Serena. Surely you know your daughter better than that."

But it was clear from this evening that she did not. And it was so odd, because he saw so many echoes of how his father had treated him in the ways Serena's mother treated her—and even more shockingly, so many similarities in how Serena got through it. For every insult against her looks, her animals, her house, she seemed to latch on to them all the harder. Just as he had to every barb that he was stupid, useless and lazy.

While he was happy to play down to any negative in-terpretations of *him*, he found he could not with deter-mined, brilliant, beautiful Serena. And so he decided to play Mrs. Valli's game for this round. Rudeness wrapped in fake concern.

"You must have loved your ex-husband very much."

She blinked, reared back almost as if she'd been struck. "What?"

"I know the marriage ended before his demise, but it is

the only way I can fathom misrepresenting your daughter in such a way. She followed his business footsteps and this hurts you in some way because you loved him and it did not work out, so you do not allow yourself to see past it." He went so far as to tut compassionately. "Losing him twice must have been quite the blow."

"Blow?" Her eyes narrowed icily. He should have seen Serena in them. They were the same shape, the same color, but there was a lack of warmth in the layers of brown and green. "I celebrated the day that useless failure of a man left this earth. I only wished he'd done it earlier."

"Mrs. Valli. That is no way to speak of the dead, or your daughter's father." And so Luciano got to his feet. "I'm afraid I cannot allow this evening to continue. I do not care for the whole of how you've treated my soon-to-be wife this evening. There will be no more invitations until you can assure me that you will be pleasant and positive toward your *only child*."

He looked briefly at Serena, who was staring at him wide-eyed and stunned. Luciano gestured to the butler. "Eduardo? Would you see Mrs. Valli out? I'm afraid Serena and I are indisposed and cannot walk her to her car ourselves."

"Serena!"

"I'm afraid this is Luciano's place, Mother," Serena said quietly. Her eyes were oddly shiny. "As polite guests, we must abide by what he says." She did not rise from her seat, so Mrs. Valli whirled on Luciano even as Eduardo came forward.

"Are you...? Do you think you're kicking me out? Do you really think—"

"I *think* it is in all of our best interests to take a pause." Luciano commended himself for his calm demeanor. Working in a club for so long had certainly taught him how to deal with the ridiculously entitled. "When you've taken a break, I hope you will come to the conclusion that you have behaved poorly, and you owe your daughter an apology. Once that is issued, I hope we can move forward more pleasantly." He managed a patient smile.

Mrs. Valli made a noise of fury. "Perhaps you both deserve each other," she ground out before jerking away from Eduardo's proffered arm and marching toward the exit herself.

Luciano tried to calm himself with a deep breath. Bullies were a dime a dozen and no doubt both he and Serena had seen their fair share. Their business was rife with them, and her father had been one just as his father had.

But something about the way her own mother had spoken of her. Like a childish adolescent trying to tear down someone who got even a scrap of attention. It was infuriating, but moreover, it was like holding up a mirror to his own adolescence and forcing him to see it through an adult lens.

Had his father really thought all those terrible things about him? Or had Luciano simply existed, soaking up attention and interest that his father preferred only on him.

He did not wish to consider it, so he turned to deal with Serena.

She stood, still as a statue and perhaps just as remote, bracketed by one floor-to-ceiling window. She watched the world outside—a soft, pastel sunset. "You did not need to stand up for me," she said after a few beats of quiet.

She sounded very…tired. Her expression was blank. A

careful mask. She did not *act* as though her mother's behavior hurt her, and yet Luciano could not shake the idea that this was how Serena would react to hurt. Cold and stony.

"It is what a fiancée would do."

"I suppose it is," she agreed. Her hazel gaze remained on the darkening world outside the large windows.

Luciano had the rare experience of not knowing what to say. So he stood next to her and said nothing. He stiffly told Eduardo he was dismissed with the kitchen staff, and that Luciano would handle everything at the apartment for the rest of the night.

Which left just Luciano and Serena and her silence.

When Serena finally broke it, it was with that careful, detached tone he knew so well. This was the one she'd always used on him in the rare occurrences their paths had overlapped over the years before she'd approached him with this plan of hers.

"Even with you standing up to her, she will never believe this is genuine, and I worry…" She swallowed, then carefully turned to face him, her gaze meeting his. He saw courage hiding something in the brown and green depths. Something like vulnerability. "I worry she won't be the only one."

Something reared inside of him. And much like the entirety of the dinner had whirled up familiar feelings in an unfamiliar setting, this did the same. Because the hint of vulnerability incited a long-buried need to fix, to *save*. When he'd been a child, he'd wanted to protect. When he'd become a teen, he'd given it up.

You could not protect those who did not wish to be protected.

No doubt Serena fell into that category. And he'd be

damned if he twisted himself in all those old knots to make the same mistake twice.

That was one thing Luciano refused to do. So, he took her words at face value, and ignored the hurt underneath.

"We don't need people to believe. In fact, doubts might help. People will be watching us. They will be intrigued. We need attention. Our names out in the ether."

"Perhaps," she agreed on a sigh. She turned her attention back to the window. "But we also need to appear like a united business front if we're hoping to woo any of our lost customers back. We want them to take the meetings because they're intrigued, but we need to close the deals because we're the best."

"Then let us be the best."

She nodded at that. No doubt a foregone conclusion for the both of them. Another heavy silence settled, though her expression was less detached and more…intense. Her lips pressed together and her eyebrows furrowed.

"Everything she said is true, you know. Or not said, but hinted at. I am dull. I like animals better than people. This ring would better suit someone like her." Serena said all these things with a certainty that irritated him. "She is not *wrong*."

Luciano could only stare at her. He didn't even fully disagree with what she was saying. But it still *grated*. Because yes, she liked animals perhaps too much. She had quirks the size of the entire country, and yes, that ring was maybe not suited to Serena's personality, but…

But Angelica Valli *was* wrong. About everything. It was clear as day to him, and it was shocking and just…wrong for that not to be clear to Serena.

It wasn't his business. None of this was an area he should insert himself into. He did not need to protect her. Serena Valli protected herself.

But she was *wrong*, and something that had broken free during that dinner whirled around inside of him, ruining his good sense to keep his mouth shut.

"*I* think she is wrong," Luciano said, too intently, no doubt. "Because in the long space of time I have known you, Serena Valli, I have never once considered you *dull*."

CHAPTER ELEVEN

Serena hated the feelings battering around in her chest. Hated that she couldn't seem to ice them away.

His fault. Half her mother's. Half his. Had to be, because she was better at dealing with the way her mother was when she was alone. When she was in her own space.

He added a new element and she *hated* it. She so desperately wanted to hate it and him and everything inside of her she couldn't control, organize or perfect.

I have never once considered you dull.

"You do not need to stand up for me," she insisted. It seemed imperative, even if she couldn't understand why, to get that through to him. Though she couldn't meet his gaze. Or even the gentle waves of the ocean as dark began to fall. She turned away from both.

She'd planned on staying, but maybe she could go and that would be okay. Maybe…

"I thought you understood, *cara*, I do not do what anyone else needs. I do what suits me. I say this because it is the truth."

The truth. When the truth never mattered. And something about the way he was acting, like he was some noble person, and not the reprobate she'd always known him to be. Like the facade of his was a lie, and underneath it all was this man who was not vapid or frivolous or careless.

How in this moment she *needed* him to be all those things she'd once thought him. She didn't understand why, but she absolutely needed the old Luciano to be the true Luciano. So she lashed out, pretending he hadn't upended everything she'd thought about him.

"How I would love to be like you, Luciano. So unconcerned with what anyone needs. Flippant about legacies and responsibilities." Because it felt like she had the weight of *everything* sitting on her chest, and he acted as if it was nothing.

He didn't outwardly react to her words. He stood there, a beautiful mountain made of stern jagged edges. She wanted him to flash one of those insouciant smiles. A dagger in its own right.

But he did nothing but speak very carefully. "I am here, am I not?" His voice was deep, cutting. A warning, and she should heed it. She always heeded warnings.

But something was exploding inside of her. And it was *his* fault, because she could always deal with her mother. Maybe sometimes the barbs landed, but mostly it was just the same old insults and they didn't matter. They were simply different people, and the great Angelica Valli would never understand understated, introverted Serena.

It was fine.

It had always been fine.

Then Luciano had created this experience where he insisted on being a witness to her mother's barbs and that had felt…

Terrible. Belittling. Embarrassing and shameful.

Even that she could have withstood with her usual fortitude. But for him to kick her mother out? Insist on an apology before anything else progressed? As though… As though this thing she had spent her childhood telling herself didn't matter, actually did.

He'd stood up for her, and she'd had to come to the startling revelation over dessert that no one ever had before.

She had clung to her grandfather because he'd understood her, given her space to be herself, but he'd never protected her from the slings and arrows of her parents. He'd told her to endure them. To create a shield through which they could not penetrate.

He had never offered to be her shield. It had never occurred to her that he should.

Until tonight. Until this man, her enemy, her rival, her soon-to-be fake husband had, in just one meeting, done what no one in her life who claimed to care ever had.

Tears stung her eyes. Unreasonable. Unfathomable. She didn't cry in public. She always, *always* willed any emotion away, but she was failing in the moment and it was awful.

She couldn't possibly stay here. She whirled away from him, blinded by those tears. Horrified by them. "I have to go." She thought nothing of her purse or how she would get home without her keys, her wallet, her anything. She only thought of escape.

She didn't even reach the entry. Luciano caught her by the arm and turned her around. He blocked the exit and held her there. So her only option was to look down at the floor and hope he didn't notice the teardrops fall and land on the soft carpet at their feet.

Because, God, how could she ever let him see a weakness, an imperfection such as this?

One of his hands came under her chin. Pressed up. She could have fought it. Could have jerked her chin away, pushed him, a million things she could have done. Instead, she let the pressure move her chin up, and she looked him in the eye, even with tears streaming down her cheeks.

She did not know what she saw in his expression, only that it thundered inside of her like a storm. Only that it made her shudder from head to toe. That it seemed to reach inside her and change the very chemistry of her being.

He brushed the wetness away with the sides of his thumbs as his hands cupped her neck. It was impossibly gentle. This man who'd represented, like his father and her own, everything she hated. Waste and foolish pride and carelessness.

Except in these short days, she'd come to accept he wasn't that man at all.

It was such a betrayal.

As was him being the only one to ever wipe away her tears.

"Come, *cara mia*. You must not cry. Particularly not on my shoes. That's expensive Italian leather."

She *almost* managed a bit of an amused sound at that, but there was nothing to be amused about. If dinner was embarrassing, this was a humiliation she did not know how to bear. *This* was why she preferred to be alone. This was why she preferred her cats. This was why her icy shields *were* important. She could be perfect there.

She could not be perfect when Luciano did not let her go. His hands on her neck, large and warm and like an anchor amidst all the chaos inside of her. A heated center point to the ice she could not seem to muster up.

"You must not let her get to you," he said, very earnestly. When she wasn't certain she'd thought him capable of earnest.

But he did not understand, and she could only blame this new *earnestness* of his for her wanting to explain it to him. "*She* does not get to me. *She* is not the problem. She is who she has always been. Selfish and, perhaps it's fair to say, mean. My father did not marry her for her warmth. I'm not entirely sure why they even bothered to have me." She shook her head. Hated that even all these years later the thought depressed her. "But I do not…base my worth on what my mother said. I would have given up on success a long time ago if I did."

"Then why do you cry?"

She sucked in a deep breath, but it didn't settle the need to get it out. A need bigger than her fear of exposing herself to an enemy.

"Has it ever occurred to you how alone you really are?" she demanded, feeling the tears return in earnest, though she furiously blinked them back. "You cannot imagine what it is like to have someone…stand up for you, and realize they are the only one who has." Her voice broke on the last few words.

"You do not mean *someone*," he said, his voice quiet and serious. "You mean someone like *me*."

"Someone who hates me," she returned, lifting her chin. Daring him to argue. She should have known better than to lay down a dare.

"I have never *hated* you, Serena." He said it with such

deep conviction that it felt as though her heart shivered inside of her chest.

"You needn't lie," she managed to rasp out. She cleared her throat, worked on getting back her armor. "I believe you once likened me to Satan. To my face."

One side of his mouth quirked up in amusement. "Perhaps I did. But that wasn't about *you*. It was what you represented. I didn't know you were a strange little cat lady when I likened you to Satan. And while I think one of those creatures of yours *might* be an evil minion sent from hell, I do not think you are."

She choked on some strange mix of a laugh and outrage. He made no sense. This actually making her feel somewhat better was baffling.

"Does it matter what I think?" he asked.

"Of course not." She didn't want it to. She didn't think it should. But his hands were still on her neck. His body was still far too close. And while she usually felt hollowed out and beat down for a few hours after dealing with her mother and refusing to cry—the crying, being comforted, was cathartic.

She should hate him for that. Or thank him. She relished neither and didn't know what to do with herself. What to say. Especially with the understanding that they were too close and didn't need to be.

She could feel his breath, mingled with hers. So close. So unnecessarily close. His hands were still on her face, holding her just there. While his gaze, dark and intent, searched hers for something. She didn't know what. She couldn't fathom what.

She shouldn't want him to find it. She shouldn't *want*

this, but her heart was beating overtime as a heat seeped into her bloodstream, spreading through her like alcohol. A drug-like softening. Until she found herself nearly melted against him, and a new, alarming pulse beat deep within. Wanting something…something only he could give.

And she knew it was wrong, this yearning. Letting him be this close. All the lines they were crossing instead of carefully adhering to. And she had always, *always* done the right thing.

But never in her life had the wrong thing been quite so tempting.

Luciano did not know what he was doing. He did not recognize himself. The violent ricochets of need rattling around inside of him. A gentleness that was either foreign or something so long lost he'd fully forgotten what it felt like inside of his body.

But there was a need wriggling through, one that was all too familiar. He tried to remember that this was all part of his plan. Seduction. Want. Need. To lull her into a false sense of security.

But it was supposed to be *her* wants and needs more than his. And he did not know how whatever was roaring through him could be matched. It was all-encompassing, consuming to the point he wasn't sure he cared about what he'd meant to do, what was important, who had the upper hand. Not if he could once again get his mouth on hers.

Which is what he did. Closed that small distance and tasted her once more. It wound like relief through him. It had only been days since that fake kiss on the beach…that hadn't been as fake as he'd like. But there was no hiding that this wasn't for potential photographers.

It was for him. *Him*.

And her, he supposed, as she sighed into him. An echo of the relief he felt inside of himself. Because thank God they both wanted this thing they shouldn't. What a disaster it would be if it were one-sided, this sizzling, warping, *thrilling* want.

She made a sound, some odd mix between a moan and distress, so he eased back.

She gripped his forearms as if to steady herself, and maybe he should have released her face. But he couldn't seem to get his brain to send out any signals to the muscles that held her still. Her mouth was swollen, her eyes wide and leaning more brown than green, her cheeks flushed.

She breathed heavily, her eyes darting from his mouth to his eyes to his mouth again. But she seemed to come to her senses before he did.

Except there was no sense in what she said.

"There's no one to pretend for, Luciano."

Damn the way she said his name. "Who said I was pretending?" he demanded on a growl, resisting—narrowly—the desire to give her a shake until she got it through her thickest of thick skulls. He should have stopped this. Should have used that sentence against her.

But something about the vulnerability he'd seen today made him incapable of being as ruthless as he should be. Something about her tears had stripped him down, and he could only offer her the truth in return.

"I want *you*, Serena."

She looked at him, those eyes wide and wet. There was

such confusion in them. Mixed with lust. "Why?" she asked on a pained whisper.

But her pain had nothing on his. That she could ask that question. That he didn't have an answer for it. "How the hell am I supposed to know?" And this time when he kissed her, he held nothing back. He let the whole war inside of him explode between them. He tasted her, deeply and selfishly. Just for him.

He half expected her to be cowed. Scared into pushing him away, into demanding he stop. Instead she met every kiss, every nip, every tightened grasp with one of her own. Dragging them both deeper into an inferno that would no doubt destroy them.

Luckily, he'd always been a fan of destruction.

He molded his hands over her shoulders, her arms, then anchored them at her waist to draw her closer. As close as she could get. A wild, desperate pressing of body against body. And her arms came around his neck, so she arched into him.

A jolt of pleasure so deep it almost mixed with pain shot through him. His body was iron hard, and she was a warm softness, begging for more.

Something incomprehensible was unfurling inside of him. None of his usual walls. There was too much emotion infiltrating that which should only be physical, light, easy.

There was nothing easy about this woman. About this kiss. He was being sucked in. Drowned. Which made no sense. *She* was the virgin. Not him.

There would come a moment where he would push her too far. Where she would want to stop. To pretend this wild loss of control had never happened. So he rushed forward to greet it. Or thought he did.

When he unzipped the back of her dress, she shrugged her shoulders to let the dress fall. She didn't even hesitate. His heart seemed to stutter in his chest, and this was what had him pulling her back, away, but whatever denials had been on the tip of his tongue died.

Her underwear was a serviceable, virginal white. It made her look like a confection. One he desperately needed a taste of. She was a goddess. Soft and enticing. No doubt luring him to his doom.

What a way to go.

They both were gasping for air. Her pupils were large and dark and a flush had crept down from her face to her chest. For a moment, he thought he saw a flicker of doubt, but before he could use it…or refute it, she stepped forward and lifted her mouth to his once more. She kissed him and her hands slid up his chest, to the buttons of his shirt. She fumbled, but she didn't give up, kissing him and unbuttoning his shirt one by one until he thought there was no sound in the world expect the sound of his own heart beating like a booming drum chorus in his ears.

His hands, without any permission from what little part of his brain he thought he still might have control over, slid down her back, over the curve of her backside. Every inch of her was soft, supple, warm.

The kiss could have gone on forever, but there was a warning bell somewhere deep down. A sense of self-preservation just barely nagging at him. Tiny, but abrasive. He wrenched his mouth from hers, alarmed at how winded he felt. This couldn't continue. This couldn't *be*.

He stared down at her, this unexpected temptress, still feeling an incomprehensible need. What would he do if she walked away?

What would he do if she did not?

Devour.

Which was wrong. It had been one thing to think of seducing her in vague terms, but the reality of wanting her was something far different. Far more alarming. Far more complex.

He was not a man who allowed for complex. He was not suited to it. He could not stand for it or dive into it like this.

"Tell me to stop," he demanded. It was the only thing that could save him. Her good sense was all that stood between them and the ruin of giving in to this. Because it wasn't seduction games.

It was something more. Something he wasn't sure either of them would survive.

"Tell me you don't want this," he demanded of her. She didn't say a thing and he wanted to yell it again until she *reacted*. Instead, he issued the order again, quietly and sternly with all the strength and control left in him. "Tell me."

She inhaled sharply, then shook her head, chin lifted. "No," she said firmly. Then she jerked his head down by the hair and crushed her mouth to his.

CHAPTER TWELVE

SERENA HAD NEVER been reckless. Never thought she would be compelled to behave in such a way. Danger was for people like Luciano, who would suffer no consequences, no qualms. People who could afford to make mistakes.

Or so she'd believed.

But everything changed tonight. She did not know how, and perhaps at some later date, when her body wasn't throbbing with a need she did not fully recognize even if she knew what it meant, she would dissect it all. Understand it all.

Despair of herself.

But for this moment, the only thing she could possibly think to do was dive down the reckless, fiery disaster of it all. Disaster felt like a revelation. Giving in felt like something she *owed* herself for once.

And what would it matter if she crashed and burned on the glorious mountain of him? Tomorrow she would wake up, still Serena Valli. Still in charge of Valli and marching her way toward a merger—marital and business—with this man. And her mistake might be there, but what would it change?

Nothing. Except she would know where all this led and how much her body could feel.

So for tonight, none of what they *were* mattered. All that mattered was his mouth, his tongue, his teeth. The way his hands streaked over her, stoking fires she had never once thought possible within herself.

She'd preferred ice to deal with her weakest emotions until this moment. Fire seemed everything now. At the end of all this, she would not be a hollowed out shell like she usually was. She would be something rising from the ashes.

Powerful.

And that's exactly what she felt. Though she was in nothing but her underwear, and he was fully dressed except for the fact his shirt was unbuttoned, it felt like *she* had brought this moment on.

This wasn't about her vague plans of letting him seduce her. Because she had not been seduced. She had not been lulled into something. She had *chosen*.

This kiss, his searing touch and wherever this led was about…whatever stirred between them that neither of them particularly wanted, clearly. Neither knew what to do with it.

So they were diving into the unknown together.

Except it wasn't fully unknown. He clearly knew what he was doing. The way his mouth dragged down her neck, causing her head to fall back. The way his hand moved over the front of her thigh, huge and hot, and she thought aiming for the most intimate part of her, only to bypass it entirely.

A game. Meant to stir, to tease, to frustrate. And if there was anything she knew how to do, it was how to match wits with her rival. She lowered her hands down the length of his torso, reveling in the impossibly defined muscle. Though she'd never even seen this man break a sweat…

He would now.

She unbuttoned his pants and grinned into his shoulder when he tensed. She took her time with the zipper but lost her train of thought when she felt her bra loosen because he'd unclasped it. He pulled it off her arms, dropped it onto the ground.

Serena's breath caught. She'd never been naked in front of a man before, and she did not know quite what to feel about being exposed this way. Except there was no hiding that the man liked what he saw. And there was really nothing her quivering muscles could have done except work exceptionally hard to keep her upright as he reached forward and cupped her breasts. A move both possessive and thrilling, sending an intoxicating jolt through her. When his thumbs brushed the taut nipples, Serena's legs nearly buckled. Would have, maybe, if he had not smoothed his hands down to her rib cage and pressed her to the wall.

All so that he could taste. His mouth, hot and foreign, feasted on her. Everything inside of her began to wind like a taut string. She wanted so many things, she did not know how to find them, how to demand them.

"Luciano." She sounded breathless and desperate and that might have bothered her if it did not prompt a rumbling sound deep in his throat, like a predatory, primal growl. The sound shot sparks through her, like she was nothing but fire and heat and wonder.

Then his finger traced the seam of her underwear. Then it wasn't tracing, it was dipping underneath the fabric and exploring a new part of her. Her head thunked back against the wall, and his laughter was dark against her neck.

"Serena," he murmured, his mouth tucked against the sensitive skin under her jaw. "I can feel how much you want me."

"Yes." With what little control she had, she reached out, placed the palm of her hand against the hard jut of his arousal against his pants. "And I can feel how much you want me."

"I suppose we are evenly matched then."

She wanted to say something—something cunning and sophisticated—but the only sound that escaped her mouth was a wordless noise, some mix of a gasp and moan. Because his finger was inside of her, sparking to life fires she had not known could exist. An all-encompassing, heady climb that had her forgetting about everything except that center point of her body.

Until something imploded within her and she shattered into crumbling rubble. It was a blooming, arcing explosion that messed with her equilibrium, because somehow the pleasure another person could bring her was better than anything she'd ever done herself.

Still shuddering, she tried to catch her breath. Still standing, pressed against a wall in the living room of his apartment. In front of huge windows.

She had lost herself, and that could be terrifying if they stopped here. If that's all that happened. He'd touched her and she'd fallen apart. How would she live with that?

She couldn't. There was no turning back. Not now. Not so close. She needed to know how it ended. She gripped his face, met his gaze. "More. Luciano. All."

Though he hesitated, he did not pretend to misunderstand her. After a halting moment, he swept her into his arms. In an impressive feat, he carried her through the penthouse and into a bedroom. The light had faded, so it was all dusk.

He laid her out on the bed, surveying her like some hulking conqueror, and she supposed later she might consider what it said about her that it sent a thrill through her. That she wanted to be conquered in every way by this man she would no doubt regret wanting.

"There will be no going back. When you think of your first, it will always be me."

It was meant to be a warning. She should take it as one. The stark way he looked at her. The planes of muscle and sinew that made up his powerful body. What could possibly come after this and compare?

Which was enough of an answer. Perhaps she would curse him, her weakness, this moment, forever.

But it might be worth it.

So she held his serious gaze. She could not to be afraid of mistakes now, not when she'd already made so many. It would be worse to hide and stand still. "Then it will always be you."

Something flared in his gaze. She wasn't sure she'd understand that emotion even if she was experienced. But he shrugged out of his shirt, revealing the impressive musculature of his arms. She had known he was strong. An impressive form of man, but she had not realized how deep that went.

He divested himself of his pants, all while she watched. And while she had read about all sorts of romantic encounters, she had no real-life scenario to compare this to. Nerves fluttered, but they weren't the kind made from worry. It was something else. Something akin to hope.

And then he pushed his boxers down, revealing the impressive hard length of him. She hated to be a cliché, but she simply did not know how that was truly meant to fit inside of her. She nearly laughed at the foolishness of the thought, but she was breathing too hard to laugh. Heated and pulsing too much to do anything but *watch*.

He pulled something out of the drawer, and she realized dimly that he must have more brain cells left than she did. He opened the condom package and rolled it on, watching her the entire time. She did not know if this was really considered an intimate act, or part of it, but she supposed it only mattered what they wanted it to be. And she could scarcely look away. It was all so new, so enticing.

To have a man move atop her, glare down at her. Hard and surely aching as much as she was. He wouldn't be doing this otherwise. Not like this.

"It may hurt," he said, his voice sounding like it was being scraped out of a closed throat.

"What a shocking revelation. I have no concept of how sex works despite my twenty-six years on this planet. Please explain it to me, Luciano." She felt him tense every time she uttered his name, so she drew it out syllable by syllable, hoping she might hear him growl again.

He made a low sound of amusement instead, but it rumbled through her all the same. Because the hard, dangerous length of him was positioned at her entrance.

Nerves fluttered around her heart, but they were the anticipatory kind. That breathless feeling before jumping into the unknown. It felt like power. A choice. *Her* choice. Everything *she* wanted.

It didn't so much *hurt* as feel impossible as he moved into her, slow and determined. A deep, uncomfortable stretching, but it was buffeted by so many wonderful sensations it was impossible to focus on that discomfort. Especially when she moved and he growled.

He liked it, she realized. Pleasure gave pleasure, and the more she relaxed into that, the less she felt as if it simply wasn't physically possible to enjoy the feel of being so stretched, so invaded.

But it wasn't just possible, it was elemental. Echoing through her, with every slow, controlled thrust. She wriggled beneath him, desperate for that climax he'd given her with his hand out in the other room. She wanted it now. So she began to meet his thrusts. Knew it was what he wanted as the muscles in his neck strained for control.

It felt wild and free. Nothing she'd ever been. Nothing she'd ever wanted. But that reckless fury in his eyes felt like everything she'd been missing. For maybe her whole life.

She came apart in panted sighs and his name on her lips. It was earthshaking. Rearranging everything she'd ever thought…if she could ever reasonably *think* again.

He held her still, there under him, as the orgasm rattled through her, eased. But he was still deep inside her. He was still here, looking down at her like she was something he could not bear to look away from.

Because he could see her. *Her.* He had gotten under her armor, her mask, and he saw her and wanted to.

She felt oddly emotional. Wanted to reach out. Wanted something she did not know how to express. A connection, somehow. Because she'd seen underneath his armor too. The way he'd talked of his father. Not the careless throw-away lines about how they didn't get along.

The cord of truth as to *why*.

She put her palm to his cheek, needing some kind of guidance for this huge thing expanding inside of her. "Luciano."

"Hush," he ordered. And then he was pulling her up. Into his lap. Sliding into her from this new angle. She nearly burst apart again in one simple thrust, everything whirling in her mind forgotten in lieu of feeling. His mouth found her breast, one hand holding her hip as the other slid up her back, then gripped her hair.

It was not pain exactly. Instead, it vibrated through her like rapture.

"You will come apart for me again, *cara mia*," he muttered in a dark, commanding voice. "Now."

The order thrilled her, and yet she couldn't resist *some* reluctance to be ordered about. "You cannot tell me what to do, *carissimo*." But she panted it, at the end of some race she couldn't fully understand, and couldn't imagine not wanting to do again. Moving against him, building that climb again. Again and again, she wanted this and him.

His laugh was dark and thrilling. He was deep inside of her. He was everything.

And she was lost.

She had stripped him of everything. Every mask he'd worn, every piece of armor he'd lovingly crafted for himself. He felt soft and weak and utterly…lost with need. Not a need for that final push, the rush off the cliff. As much as he wanted that, he did not *need* it as much as he needed her in his arms.

It was inexplicable and problematic and horrible, and still she was so warm and pliant against him. And still she had breathed his name like a prayer. And *still* all he wanted was this, knowing all the ways it could not, would not, work in his favor. It wasn't even a tactical error at this point, it was simply catastrophe.

Understanding that did nothing to stop his enjoyment of her. The lavender smell that had infiltrated his bed. The soft, sweet give of her skin. She was perfect from head to toe. The pleasured sleepiness in her hazel eyes a kind of drug he could not imagine finding elsewhere.

"Now it is your turn," she murmured. "You will come apart for me."

"Will I?"

She made a sound low in her throat, then she moved against him, clearly testing. When he sucked in a breath through his teeth, her grin was self-satisfied and gorgeous. What an unexpected siren she was.

And since she was, he let her take over, with her teasing moves, her careful strokes, her breath fluttering against his sweat-slicked skin. Her breasts brushed against his chest, and every time she sighed, it was in pleasure. Because she was building herself up again. Finding what she liked along with him.

He let her. He tried to let her. Until he could not control it because she was tightening around him yet again, breaking that last grip on his command. He moved her onto her back and thrust home one last obliterating time. The climax exploded in a preternatural burst of pleasure that made very little sense to him. That something he had done many a time could feel different and unique and *important*.

He would deal with that later. When he could breathe. When he could see. When he came down from whatever high he was on. When he could find the sense to roll off her.

It should have come when she stroked a hand down his back, then up again, as if to comfort. It should have come when she gently raked her fingers through his hair.

It was such a soft, gentle gesture that everything inside of him tensed. Iced. A strange niggle of something that felt like *fear* chased through him.

Her hand slipped from his hair. Her expression grew grim. But she did not look away.

"Well," she said. "I suppose that is done."

But everything in him, no matter the fear or the ice, rejected that sentiment. Because *no*. No. It wasn't *done*.

"Not yet."

CHAPTER THIRTEEN

SERENA AWOKE IN a strange bed, in a strange room dimly lit by the faint glow of daylight coming through a corner of the window.

Alone. In a room that smelled like Luciano's expensive cologne.

She took a slow, careful inhale, trying not to catalogue the way her body felt. If she could be still in her mind, *feelings* wouldn't start infiltrating her decision making.

And *boy* did she have some decisions to make.

It was good to be alone. It gave her a moment to come to terms with all that had changed. Because as much as she'd like to be cosmopolitan enough to pretend as though this had just been a fun one-off, all that lingered in their future was not *fun*.

And she had to know how to proceed before she faced him.

Maybe she wouldn't have to face him at all. Maybe he was so embarrassed he'd left fully. She half wanted it to be true, half felt bereft at the thought.

Surely if he was *that* embarrassed, he wouldn't have turned to her in the night. He wouldn't have gruffly told her she wasn't going anywhere when she had suggested she return home, late into the evening.

Surely.

But maybe it was the heat of the moment talking. And now that the heat had cooled into the morning after, he felt... Oh, she didn't know.

She squeezed her eyes shut, focusing on breathing. She was not and had never been a catastrophizer. She dealt with problems coolly, rationally. She wasn't going to sit here and panic over uncertainty. Over what a man might feel or not feel here in the aftermath of what they'd done to each other.

Because it didn't matter what *he* felt. It mattered what she did. And here in this moment alone, she needed to decide what that was and how to go forward. Only once she was sure of herself would it matter what was on *his* mind.

Sex had been revelatory. She didn't *relish* that realization, but it was true so there was no use denying it. Would it feel that way with anyone else? She had concerns it would not. There was something too...elemental about Luciano. About who he was and how he saw her.

It did not fully make sense, but in so many ways, the past week of working together had begun to show how much they were alike. There were still many differences, but there was so much core similarity, it was almost as if they *complemented* each other when they wanted to, rather than opposed each other.

Of course, that was neither here nor there either. The question was, how would this move forward with Luciano? He was the crux of her business plan moving forward. Which also involved him becoming her husband. So perhaps sex was simply...part of that. Perhaps, no matter how it had felt, it didn't *need* to be a big deal. It could be something they indulged in when they felt like it. Like an overly rich dessert.

She considered that for a few moments. Was it sensible? Or did she just want to feel him inside her again and that was clouding her judgement? She wasn't sure, because her judgement had never truly been clouded before.

She really wished she had one of her notebooks. She could create a pro and con list. She could remind herself of her goals, center herself on the mission statement she'd created for this little plot.

Never lose sight of what's best for Serena Valli.

Before she could make any decisions about what last night meant for that, the door to the bedroom opened. Serena tucked the sheet under her chin and watched as Luciano appeared carrying a tray full of food. She hadn't realized until this moment just how hungry she was. Hadn't thought to concern herself with how late in the morning it might be.

"You're awake. Wonderful. Here is breakfast," he offered, keeping his gaze on the tray as he settled it into the middle of the large bed. It was full of breakfast pastries, a selection of fruits, yogurt and a carafe of coffee.

"Help yourself to whatever suits," he said with a sweeping gesture, standing there at the side of the bed.

She studied the offerings and selected a decadent *bomboloni*. Not her usual choice for breakfast, but today seemed to call for decadent and sweet. Maybe come Monday she would reset herself. Get back to reason and good choices.

"Coffee?" Luciano asked.

"Please," she agreed, then watched him as he poured two mugs of coffee and handed her one.

He didn't sit on the bed, or any of the other seating in the room. Instead he stood and sipped. He was acting…a little odd. Awkward wasn't the right word. She wasn't sure Luciano could ever be awkward. But there was a strange stiffness to him, as though this was as new a territory for him as it was for her.

She might not have thought that possible, and she did not know about his romantic history, but she knew he hadn't been fake-engaged to any of his previous lovers. So there were strange, new and complicated elements this morning that they both found themselves in.

She mulled this over as she ate and drank her coffee. Last night, she had felt powerful. Equal to whatever Luciano gave. She had not *expected* that to be the case, but it was. And now, it was the same. Because, no matter how many *mornings after* he'd encountered, *this* was something else.

She did not *smile* at the thought, but she wanted to. Still, she doubted he saw this in the exact same way.

So, she needed to approach this as she approached anything else. With a carefully thought out plan. If nothing else, they *did* work well together—in and out of the bedroom—no matter what a surprise that was.

"I suppose we must discuss the events of last night," she ventured, wondering how he would take that since he wasn't the one introducing the topic.

"I suppose we must," he agreed neutrally.

She wanted to frown at him, but she focused on the pastry and tried to decide where to start. But perhaps *start* was the key, because for as much as she'd enjoyed it, she wasn't sure she understood it. "Why did it happen?"

"Well, if you recall, I gave you many outs and you did not take them."

She sighed heavily. He was being purposefully obtuse, and she did not care for it. Except she thought it meant that it must matter to him in *some* way, or he would be more... dismissive or superficial. He would be leading this discussion. He would be blustering and telling her what's what.

But it was her leading the charge, which meant he was just as much in the dark about how to move forward as she was. It was comforting and allowed her to settle back into the pillows and enjoy finishing off her pastry as she tried to consider the facts of the matter over the feelings from last night *and* this morning.

"You did not have to kiss me," she said carefully. "While I don't care to cry in front of others and avoid it as much as possible, I have never been kissed in response to tears."

His grunt was irritable, and it always—even now—felt like a bit of a personal victory when she could be the one irritating him.

He offered no response to her, so she kept talking. "Perhaps this all makes sense to you, but it makes none to me, and I am trying to...understand it so we can decide where to go from here. But you will have to be more forthcoming."

"It is not complex, Serena. You are a beautiful woman." He smiled at her, and she knew she was meant to see that arrogant charm, but there was something darker underneath it, the edges of that deep frown still flickering in his expression. Even as he delivered the rest. "And I am a handsome man."

She could leave it at that. Perhaps she would be smart to. But he was here. He could walk out of this room, end this conversation. Maybe he wanted to be difficult, but he didn't seem eager to end it.

"It's more than simple attraction."

His expression was grim. His entire body rigid. "I did not expect you of all people to romanticize things, Serena. No one said you have to like a person to have good sex, *cara*. Surely even you know this."

That was the trouble. She was starting to like him. Or respect him. Or *something* more than the easy disdain she'd once had for him. That was when he'd been nothing more than a caricature to her. Now he was a man. Not perfect by any means, but far more complicated than she'd ever have given him credit for without spending time with him.

For instance, she could see he was *trying* to be insulting. Which was simply a distancing mechanism, not an actual belief he had. Because he was so far off base, she couldn't find offense. Romanticize? Romanticizing the situation would be dreaming about real *I do*s and *happily-ever-after*s.

She was simply trying to figure out how to ensure that sex—or this *like* and *respect* for him that was creeping up on her against her will—didn't affect their bottom line.

"Perhaps this is true," she said carefully. Arguing with him wouldn't change what he thought. "But I think we recognize something in each other. That is not romantic. It is a reasonable observation based on the events of the past week. And I think it's imperative we understand it, lest we…make mistakes moving forward. Mistakes that hurt what's most important."

He stared at her then. His gaze hard. Not even a flicker of warmth or kindness in their dark depths.

"And to you, what's most important is a business."

He said this with some disdain, which was rich, coming from him.

"A legacy, Luciano," she corrected. "Mine. And yours. The whole reason we spent more than five minutes in a room together, in fact."

"I see. So you want to analyze it. Perhaps make some data points in one of your little notebooks. How did it come to be that you were swept away by a cad like Luciano Ascione?"

She considered the snap in his tone. The way he called himself a cad, when she hadn't been thinking that at all. He gave himself away when he let his temper rule, so she could not deny that she continued to poke at that temper in a way she knew would annoy him the most.

Remain calm and controlled and focused on the facts alone. "I would not call you a cad in this instance."

He snorted with disgust. "In this instance," he said, in a mocking tone. "I would think you a robot if not for last night," he muttered.

"I truly don't understand why you're angry, Luciano. We had a pleasurable evening. It is a complication, but one I think we can reasonably maneuver if we discuss it like adults."

She thought she was being the *most* reasonable and adult, but clearly he did not agree. *He* looked like he was about to throw a temper tantrum.

So she settled into the pillows even deeper and tried not to smile.

She was infuriating. He'd woken up, tied in knots he didn't understand. He could not untangle them, even in the time he'd taken away from her sleeping soundly in *his* bed, *his* room, *his* life.

And she was sitting there eating a pastry in his bed trying to *understand*. Wanting to have a calm discussion. *Smiling* at him, like she was the queen of the world in control of everything, and he was a foolish serf, stomping his foot in defiance.

What was calm about what had occurred? What was *reasonable* about anything? He could not make sense of the way she'd tangled inside of him like a poisonous vine.

She wanted to discuss *sex* like adults. She wanted reasons. She wanted truths.

Well, fine. He'd give them to her. All the hard truths she wouldn't want to hear. All the truths that, if she were as smart as she allegedly was, would send her running.

"Do you know, last night as I watched your mother play her little games, I had the most startling realization that I'd seen it all before?"

She studied him silently, clearly not following but not willing to say that. Her smile had dimmed though. She definitely hadn't expected him to bring up her mother.

"You see, I recognized something in the way your mother treated you," he continued. "Because she was wrong, and I could not fathom what would be the reason for a mother to lie about their child."

She blinked, gathered that sheet a little closer to her chest, all traces of that smile gone.

"It reminded me of my own childhood dinners. At the time, I was not old enough to realize that every night, my father was playing his favorite game. He would insist my mother dine with us, then treat her terribly until she ran off in tears, then insist we do the same thing the next night. He enjoyed that—something I understood even as a small child, even if I did not understand why."

He had begged his mother to refuse to show. He had tried to chase after her, only to be rejected by her. He had tried, as he'd gotten older, to convince her to leave. He had tried so many things, but his father had been the center of everything in that house.

And Gianluca Ascione had known it.

"Once he'd finally gotten her to break, he would turn to me. Just as your mother turned to you last night. Different insults, naturally, but the same tactic. He thought me stupid, or claimed he did. He characterized me as the character I would then become. I knew he was wrong. For a while, I thought it was a mistake. I would simply prove it to him. Then I realized I could not. But I never understood why, when I *knew* I was not what he claimed I was, most days. Until I saw your mother. Doing the same thing. And it was wrong, but I have no doubts about you, so I *knew* it was wrong on a deeper level."

Serena's expression was growing icy. He told himself that's what he wanted, even as it settled in him like pain.

"She was not fully wrong," she said in that careful, horrible way.

"That's rubbish," he spat. "She wants you to be those things—dull and foolish—because admitting you are all the things you *actually* are—beautiful and certainly quirky, but not foolish—would be intimidating to her. She wants all the attention, all the good for herself. You are a…threat, I suppose."

She wasn't so icy now. She was breathing a little heavily,

color in her cheeks, the sheet clutched so tight in one hand her knuckles were white. "My mother is far more beautiful and worldly than I am. Which is fine, because I do not need to be those things."

"Even if I agreed, it doesn't matter. At the heart of her, what I witnessed last night was blatant insecurity. And instead of looking at you as your own person, or someone to be proud of, she sees you as a symbol of what she isn't. Young and brilliant and successful."

She looked completely and fully arrested by this very true description of herself, and he wanted to crawl into that bed and cover her body with his and think of nothing but the pleasure they could give each other.

That would be easy and, by God, that was what he wanted. What he'd always wanted. So why he stood here and kept talking, he'd never fully understand.

"And in the middle of that dinner, I realized that my entire childhood was simply that. Enduring the insults of an insecure man who was afraid I might be better, or more interesting, or more worthy of the attention he might someday get. Trying to save a woman who would rather be the victim of that than stand up for herself."

Stand up for me.

And he had not saved his mother. He had never gotten through to her, never protected her, never turned himself into something more powerful than his father. "She did not wish to be saved by the likes of me, and perhaps that was her right. It is your right."

She looked up at him then, and something there in her hazel eyes sent a bolt of fear through him. That everything would change now that she knew him. Saw him.

Now that she had showed him this softer side of herself. Not just the heat behind the ice, but the warmth, the soft spots he'd once been so sure he'd expose and use…

Now she had some twisting power over him instead. He had been drunk on actually saving her and now he was drunk on that look in her eyes. Soft. Vulnerable. *Mine.*

"No one has ever stood up for me before. Not like that."

He did not want to hear that. It was a power that was too big. Too much. She would come to realize, as everyone did, that he was no one's savior. And then where would they be?

But he had stepped in and saved Serena last night from some small piece of hurt. Clearly, it had caused him to lose his damn head. Because she now knew more about his inner workings than anyone else in his entire life. It left him feeling exposed and vulnerable and disgusted with himself.

Perhaps his father hadn't been jealous, but right. Because if Luciano was *smart*, he would have unveiled none of that to her. His enemy. His rival. The woman who he would someday certainly betray.

She sighed and finally looked away. At the windows, even though the drapes hid any view out of them. He could not begin to imagine what she was thinking about, but he found himself bracing for it all the same. Because somehow he knew… He knew it would be too close to a truth he did not wish to acknowledge.

"We are alike, it seems," she said quietly, her gaze still on the drapes. "More alike than different when all is said and done."

He refused to respond, but it didn't seem to matter. She kept talking.

"I knew… I do not think my mother is fully wrong about

me, per se. In her world, I *am* dull and not as beautiful. This is not an…insult to me. It is simply a fact. I… I like what I like. I am who I am. It is hard sometimes to harden myself against the way she wants to belittle me in front of others, but I might be able to weather it better with your interpretation of her behavior, because I think you are right. She is insecure." She gave a little nod, as if it would solidify the truth of the statement.

But he could see the tears starting to collect in her eyes. Particularly as she continued to speak.

"It seems… That we both did the same thing in response to these people in our lives. We created characters." Her gaze moved back to him, shiny but direct. "But we did not fully believe them to be true because we knew ourselves well enough not to."

A revelation he did not want thundered through him. He certainly didn't want to share it with *her*, when everything about her was already too damn confronting. So he did not touch that truth with a ten-foot pole.

"For the love of all that is holy, you will not cry again."

She lifted her chin. "I shall cry whenever I like."

But she didn't. She blinked the tears away, sitting in the middle of his bed, looking like a queen—royal and in charge.

"Perhaps there are more similarities than we first conceived of, but that changes nothing." He said this firmly, wishing he believed it.

She nodded, which felt like a dagger to the heart. A heart he didn't want. Wouldn't accept. A heart got a man nowhere.

"I suppose we should avoid complications then."

He agreed, wholeheartedly, but couldn't get his mouth to work. She moved her hazel gaze back to him again, studied him in that way of hers. It spoke of that brilliance she had, but there was warmth under it.

An understanding that he didn't want under it.

She moved to the side of the bed, the sheet moving off of her. He should not watch the smooth silk of her skin come into view, but he could not help himself. She walked toward him, completely naked, her hair a compelling mass of waves around her shoulders. There was nothing but confidence in her stride, and she never once let her gaze dip from his.

A challenge. Not just to him. But to his words. Even though she'd agreed.

He refused to clear his throat, so his words were rasped. "My thoughts exactly. This is complicated enough, after all."

She gestured behind him, to a chair where he'd settled her discarded dress from last night. "I believe that's my dress. If you'll move or hand it to me."

She was only inches away from him. Naked and perfect. Not an inch of embarrassment or carefulness in her gaze.

She was doing it on purpose. Testing him. Teasing him. *Something.* When he'd seen plenty of naked women in his life. He had had amazing sex. He had been there and done that and she wasn't special.

He didn't want her to be special. He didn't want her to tempt him. Why should she tempt him? He should be stronger than that.

But he wasn't.

CHAPTER FOURTEEN

THEY DID NOT avoid complication. They reveled in it. They did not have another serious conversation about what they were doing. They went forward with business plans and wedding plans in full force.

They spent too much time together. Every night. Mostly at her place, but sometimes at his if their business meetings went late.

Serena recognized this was too much—especially without a serious, adult conversation on what it meant. She always told herself, when she was alone, that she would do something about it. That they would sit down and discuss what they were really doing. She'd never been in a relationship before, but she knew a conversation was needed, and she would need to be the one to instigate it.

But she never did.

She kept waiting for *him* to do something about it. To reject her. To distance himself. Surely he'd get bored.

But he never did.

Being around him was…she hesitated to use the word *addicting*, but it was certainly something similar. Because she had never realized just how lonely she'd been. Even when her grandfather had been alive. He had been so much to her, but he had been an old man. In some ways, his wisdom and his acceptance of her quirks served as almost everything good in the foundation of her life.

But that didn't mean she hadn't been starved for companionship her own age. Her own stage in life. Someone to grow…with. And that's what this felt like. As she and Luciano tackled business problems together. As they went out to business dinners or just to be seen. As they spent every night together. To the point where she had begun ruminating on her choice of whether or not to get a house dog out loud to him.

She didn't think he actually *listened*, and she didn't think she needed him to. It was just nice to have a living and breathing sounding board, even when it was silent.

But he didn't remain silent.

"Why do you not just buy the damn dog then?" he demanded one sunny weekend afternoon as they drank lemonade on her balcony. She was on her computer, looking at pictures on the breeder's website. She'd though he was taking a nap.

But his gaze was on her now. Frustration mixed with amusement in his gaze. And since there was some amusement, she posed her concern.

"What if he doesn't get along with Kate and Leopold?"

"*Mio Dio*, Serena. This is madness. Buy the dog or do not. You must make a decision and *move on*."

Somewhat stung, she sniffed. "I only started considering the dog because Pierro said no to the bird."

"The man has sense. You? I am not so sure about. Can't you go…meet the furry creature with your demon spawn in tow to find out if they get along?"

"I suppose I could ask," she murmured thoughtfully. Both because it was a good idea and because for all his bristle, he didn't seem *opposed* to another *demon spawn* traipsing about.

She made the appointment for the next day and was shocked when he insisted on driving her out to the breeder's estate. He grumbled the entire way, warily eyeing the cats in their carrier in the back of his car. But he went.

And he was kind and charming to the breeder. He even let the puppy chew on his laces without any complaint. And when he knelt down and stroked the puppy's soft, silky ears, and a small smile appeared on his face, she couldn't help but tease him a little.

"It's official," she'd said as the dog tried to climb up Luciano's leg.

He lifted his gaze, sobered his expression and raised an eyebrow at her. "What is?"

"You don't hate animals. You're just a dog person more than a cat person."

His mouth turned downward, though not into an all-out frown. He looked down at the dog. Then he simply grunted.

When she put down a deposit to bring home the puppy when he was old enough in a few weeks, he offered no approval or disapproval, but Serena couldn't help but believe he was pleased. That he would *enjoy* having a dog around.

When they returned to the castle, he hefted the cat carrier himself, all the way upstairs, and even undid the door to let Kate and Leopold free.

Something strange battered her chest then, but she did not fully realize what it was. Or maybe she didn't let herself put a name to it then and there. Perhaps it was too big or too scary and her brain needed time to wake up.

Because one morning she woke, tangled up in him as she usually was, and realized it was the week of their wedding.

Joy spurred through her. Anticipation and excitement. Not for the event itself, but for the fact they would be husband and wife.

And she finally realized she'd made a serious mistake.

Because she had been humming over the last-minute alterations to her dress the week before. She'd been dreaming of the way he'd look at her when she walked down the aisle of the historic church they'd picked out together. She was thinking about giving him a small say in the naming of her puppy when she was able to bring him home.

She was not daydreaming about mergers or ways she would push him out once she had some sway in Ascione. She was dreaming about *romantic* things, just as he'd once accused her of.

So it dawned on her, as he slept soundly with his arms wrapped tight around her, that she'd fallen in love with him. His humor. The way he buried all his caretaker tendencies under a sharp edge. Like he was protecting himself from something, and it made her desperate to find out what.

She would need to find out what, she supposed, but for right now she was so startled by how foolish she could be—and how wonderful it felt—that she spent a few days weighing this feeling. She continued watching him and tried to determine if he might feel the same.

They had not discussed anything of weight since their first morning after, but they still spent time together. They still worked on business together. He supported her, in small ways, at work. She tried her hand at homemaking for someone and thought…maybe, just maybe, he enjoyed it.

They all but lived together. In every single way, they behaved as a real couple. In public. In private.

Except one very important thing. They did not discuss what was happening. Where it could lead. They did not acknowledge the *truth* of what was happening between them. In some ways, they both pretended like it was still a fiction, even though it was the most real relationship she'd ever had.

Still, it was missing something important. She did not know his feelings on love. Futures. Real futures—the kind with commitment and children. She was not opposed to asking him, but she supposed there was a selfish part of her that wanted to be sure they were married first.

So Valli-Ascione wouldn't suffer.

So he couldn't run away that easily.

If she felt any guilt over this, she refused to give it the time of day. A woman had to protect herself and her legacy in whatever ways she could. Loving him did not mean she should put herself at risk.

She had to remind herself of this too often. Their wedding was in three days. She would keep it to herself for three more days.

"What do you suppose I should name the puppy when we get him?" Serena asked one night, curled up on the couch together. She dropped the casual *we* and wondered if he would stiffen.

He didn't.

He acted as though the casual intimacy was nothing, but to her it was…everything. Everything she never considered she might have. Her head in his lap, his fingers trailing through her hair as he read e-mails on his phone.

"Perhaps another name from that terrible movie you made me watch," he said, surprising her with any suggestion at all, let alone one so…perfect. "Keep it all on theme."

The movie was not terrible. It was her favorite. But he had watched it last night and put together that the cats were named after the main characters. It was the silliest thing to want to cry over him understanding that *themed* names would appeal to her. Tears pricked her eyes anyway.

"I…" The words were ready to erupt, but they stuck there in her throat before she could utter them. She couldn't say it once his gaze moved from his phone to her.

She saw the wariness creep into his eyes, clear as day, like he could see the love in her eyes clear as day as well. So she didn't say it. She swallowed the words down. Where they belonged. At least until they were married and the businesses were fully merged.

Once she was protected, maybe…just maybe, she could let it all out. But she couldn't do it now. Still, it didn't mean she wanted to shut him out. No, she wanted him any way she could get him, and she didn't really care if it was pathetic.

"Take me to bed," she murmured.

And he did. No wariness involved.

Luciano felt nothing but unsettled the closer it got to their wedding day. Because what had once felt like it could be nothing but a farce now felt…too real. He had been avoiding that reality for days now, but the closer the actual ceremony became, the less he could seem to hold it at bay.

They seemed to spend every second together, and when they weren't together, he wanted to be with her. He found himself *obsessed*, and not just with her body, but also with her mind, with her strange quirks.

The joy she'd exuded the day she'd put money down on that ridiculous dog. How she had almost cried when he'd created a silly little countdown to Stuart the dog's pickup day. How she teased him for being as excited as she was.

He could not quite understand the appeal of *cats* with their slinky eyes and snooty attitudes, but when he'd told Serena that, she'd said that it was simply because he was too much *like* them to like them. He'd wanted to be affronted.

He hadn't quite managed, because he knew in Serena's world, any comparison to an animal she loved was a great compliment. He lived for a compliment from her. They were never lies, never superficial.

She did not have either in her.

And the horrible truth was that he *did* feel some excitement about bringing a puppy home. He had never been able to have animals before. His parents did not enjoy them, and then he'd assumed himself too adult, too busy to keep them.

Serena had showed him otherwise, and there was something…just *something* about the idea of walking an animal around, enjoying its exuberance in their home—*her* home—as he'd enjoyed it on their visit.

But it wasn't just her softness he was obsessed with. The *real* Serena she let out only at home. He also appreciated the business side of her. The icy, curt way she'd cut one of her managers down to size the very next morning when he dared suggest the merger was a mistake.

She was alarmingly amazing, and he recognized this

feeling growing inside of him as an old, dangerous one he'd put away. He'd stopped yearning for his parents' affection and learned to do without. Because he was strong. Because he was purposeful. Because he did not *need* those people who had refused to see him.

Love him.

But the need winding its way around his heart when it came to Serena was too much. He couldn't seem to cut it off.

And he didn't know which prospect was worse. That the soft light in her hazel eyes—the way she sighed his name, the way she looked at him sometimes, seriously and intently—might mean she felt the same.

Or that he was delusional. That it was an act. That he was desperate for any affection and reading into things. That everything his father had once said about his intelligence about business *and* people was true. That one day Serena would look at him with tears in her eyes and turn him away, because there was nothing he could *do* right.

He didn't stop this though. Because they were getting married tomorrow. Because this was business. Because this *wasn't real*.

Not real, no matter how soft her gaze seemed to be. No matter how much taking her to bed each and every night was a glorious and never ending source of enjoyment. No matter how much the past few weeks had begun to feel like a *life* he'd never known he'd wanted.

Calm. Cozy. Serene. *Real*.

Because the want was insidious and deep inside him—the want to make it real. To be her husband. To love her. To build a life.

The knowledge he could not. Because he did not know what a real marriage looked like. What a real husband did. He wouldn't be good enough. It was *impossible*.

He remembered all too well what it was like to want something out of his control. His father's approval, his mother's love. Other people's feelings were not concrete, and they could change with the whims of time. He had no control over them.

And so he'd gone along these last few weeks, waiting for his own whim. Waiting for something to change. To feel suffocated. To find some flaw in her.

For her to finally, *finally* realize that all of the many flaws in him were not charming or acceptable at all.

But nothing changed. She simply got her hooks deeper and deeper into him. She simply settled into a life in which they were in each other's space constantly. Drowning in each other. With neither of them sensible enough to escape to shore.

Maybe she had even convinced herself that she was in love with him. He saw the way she looked at him sometimes. The way she opened her mouth to say something, then closed it as if she was afraid to say the words.

When she was never afraid. Which meant it was all wrong. Wrong. How could he exist in a place where Serena Valli was afraid? It had to be his fault somehow.

He glanced over at where she stood over the stove, humming as she cooked them dinner. Something she apparently liked to do. She was more than adept at it, and he enjoyed watching the pleasure in her expression when he enjoyed what she'd made.

Her hair was piled up on her head, and she wore casual

sweats he knew would be almost as soft as she was under his hands.

The desire to touch her—to lose himself in *her* rather than the way the anxious, horrible dread kept drifting over him and pulling him under this strange wave of…fear—was overpowering.

He never considered himself afraid, but she made him so. She made everything *so*. But if he lost himself in her now, they would be married tomorrow.

Married.

He wanted to believe it could be like this. The past few weeks. The *ease* of it. But didn't he know better?

He had watched what his parents had done to one another. He had heard Serena's own mother berate a dead man. What were they doing? What made them think they could do this?

It isn't real.

But it was. It was real, and there was no more time to pretend it hadn't become so. So, he had two choices.

He could forget every lesson he'd ever learned and try to make something work. He could believe and be crushed. He could let this destroy them both, as it no doubt would.

Or he could find his wits, his smarts, and do the right thing.

The thing that would save them both.

She was the only person he'd ever successfully saved. He could not continue on this path without saving her one last time.

And suddenly, watching her hum as she cooked them dinner, he realized what must be done. It was reckless. Shortsighted.

Necessary.

He stood from the chair he'd been sitting in abruptly. "I'm going to my club tonight," he announced, perhaps a bit overloud and out of the blue. "I have business to attend to."

"Would you like me to join you?" she asked, still focusing on whatever she was making in the skillet in front of her.

For a moment, he stared at her back. *Join you*. Yes, that was what he *would like*. Her. By his side. In his bed. Forever and ever. Smiling at him, cooking for him, crooning over her animals and making her incessant lists. He wanted her lavender scent surrounding him for all his days.

A want so bone deep he knew he would never have it. Something would change. Something would break. He would turn her away, or she would turn him away.

They would destroy each other, just as their fathers once had.

He could not live under the fear of it. Maybe fear made him a coward, but he saw it differently. He was saving her. He would *save her*. Once and for all.

So, he would not be touching her. Not tonight. Not again. If she would not be the one to call it, he had to be.

"No." The refusal was harsh and sharp. Enough that he saw the way she subtly flinched at his blunt response. "It would be a distraction," he said, though he should have left it at sharp and harsh. "I have some things that must be done before the wedding and honeymoon."

Her shoulders were stiff, and he waited for some argument. Something cutting. He waited, perhaps even hoped for, some kind of *fight*. A fight would be clear cut. A fight would be easy.

But all she said was, "All right."

It stabbed like a knife all the same. Her easy acceptance. The understanding in her eyes that she refused to acknowledge there between them.

Then again, so did he.

So they stood staring at each other, both afraid to say the things that needed to be said. Because they were alike, and maybe too much so.

"Are you going to eat before you go?" she asked blandly, some of that old ice he hadn't seen in weeks now seeping into her tone.

Guilt tried to take root inside his chest, but he refused to let it. "No. Thank you." He moved away from the kitchen, toward the exit. He had to get out. He had to change the trajectory of all of this.

And he knew… He knew just how he could do it. What would be best for all of them. He would save her.

"Luciano." Her voice was firm, chilly and it brooked no argument.

He stopped at the exit. He didn't want to look at her, but when she said nothing, he felt like he had to.

Her gaze was direct, but not icy. There was that softness he hadn't imagined Serena Valli capable of *before*, though now he realized that was the real core of her. Under all that frigid perfection was this gloriously sweet and caring woman. How she could be both the harsh businesswoman and the softhearted animal lover, completely unafraid to be herself in private, made zero sense to him.

It twisted him into a million knots, and a man could not live with these knots choking him. He could not live with the expectation of a woman like her upon him.

He would never, ever meet it.

So he would save her. He would save her from this. It became a mantra in his head, repeating. If he ran. If he broke it all, she would be free and saved.

"We're getting married tomorrow," she said, very seriously.

He looked at her. She was beautiful. Wonderful. Soft and lovely. So damn smart it hurt. He wanted her. Every night. Every day.

And he could not think of a single positive thing that could come from this. She would betray him, and he would be a fool. He would fail her, and she would be destroyed.

He would drive her from that dinner table in tears someday, like his father had done to his mother.

She would send him away someday, like his mother had done to him.

She would see him for what he really was, because it was certainly not worthy of *her*, whatever he was, whoever he was.

It wasn't good enough for *this*.

Besides, there were no forevers in this world, and he would rather ensure *now* that he did not believe in any, rather than make this worse.

For the both of them.

Still, he managed to respond. "Yes, we are getting married tomorrow," he said hoarsely. "Perhaps I will stay at the club tonight. Is it not bad luck to spend the night together before a wedding?"

She was very still and quiet for a long few moments. Her eyes were steady on his but he saw…too many things in their dark depths. "I suppose I've heard that. Then I will just…see you at the wedding tomorrow? Our wedding."

He didn't miss the way she clarified that, the way she watched him, as if she could see inside his tangled brain and make sense of what he couldn't.

It made him desperate to run, but he didn't. Because she did not call him on it. If he was a coward, so was she.

Still, he answered her. "Yes."

Then he walked away. *Walked.* Purposefully, and perhaps with some speed, but it was not a run. He did not run away.

When it's important, you do.

He shoved that thought away, the disturbing fact it sounded like Serena's voice in his head. An accusation that buried deep and sharp but proved to him he was doing this right.

I will save you.

He called his lawyer on the way. He arrived at his club, but ignored all greetings and went straight to his office. When his lawyer arrived, he said it plain. "I would like to change our arrangement."

"I knew the marriage part of this was ridiculous," the man muttered unwisely. "I can meet with the Valli lawyers tomorrow and—"

"No. I want everything signed over to Serena Valli now. No marriage necessary."

"Mr. Ascione, you can't just…"

"I can. I will. Whatever it costs, it must be done by tomorrow."

"Mr. Ascione…"

"Is there a problem? Should I call someone else who can handle the task?" he demanded.

The lawyer shook his head, began to back out of the

room. "O-of course not. You will need Ms. Valli to sign off on it as well."

"She will."

The lawyer swallowed and nodded. "All right. It shouldn't require overmuch. Would you like me to deliver the papers to her when they are done?"

It was tempting. So damn tempting. She could sign the papers with this man, and no doubt her team of lawyers, and he would not need to be involved. He would never have to see her again. He would not have to deal with the fallout.

He could fly off to London tomorrow. Tokyo. New York. Anywhere but in the same country as *her*.

But he was too much of a businessman to think that would work. To end this, to truly stop what had spiraled out of control, he could not let someone else do his dirty work.

"No. I will deliver them."

And then he would say good-bye to whatever strange interlude this had been and go back to the man he had to be.

The caricature only Serena had ever seen behind.

But she would be saved, and that was all that could matter.

CHAPTER FIFTEEN

SERENA GOT READY for her wedding day essentially alone. Oh, there was the woman who did her hair, her makeup. The wedding planner helped her into her dress, buttoning up the back and babbling nervously.

Luciano had not arrived yet.

The wedding planner assured Serena that it was okay. That they were in touch with him and other such nonsense.

But Serena knew. She'd known last night. There had just been something about the way he'd behaved. Fidgety and strange. The spell of the past few weeks broken.

She did not know why. If she looked too deeply at it, she thought she might crumble, and if there was one thing she could not do it was that. She had never crumbled. Not once. She could not let Luciano Ascione be the reason she did so now.

Perhaps that was why she could not seem to stop the motion forward. It would be less embarrassing to call it all off now, before she put the dress on, before someone—some *stranger* had to come break the news to her.

He wasn't coming. She felt it in her bones. She *knew* it.

And yet she couldn't seem to call it off. Couldn't seem to save herself the upcoming embarrassment. It was like she had to go through it, in the absolute worst way, or she might be tempted to forgive him.

Not that he'd ask for her forgiveness or want it.

She did not know what had changed. She wanted to believe it had been a bit of cold feet he'd get over. Drink it away and he'd come back in the morning with declarations of love.

That had been the romantic inside of her, and she'd known better than to believe in it. But she'd hoped in spite of herself.

Because she loved him. Loved their life.

She did not know what spooked him about that. What had changed his mind? What had *scared* him? Because she knew he *was* scared. Someday, she would think about it. Someday, she would make sense of it.

Today, she couldn't seem to. There was too much stupid, pointless yearning that she only had herself to blame for. Her mother had always told her she was dull. Never enough.

Serena should have believed her.

So she settled into the old ice. The old frigid detachment. Move one step at a time, calmly and rationally, so that when he didn't show, this horrible love inside of her would crack into dust and die.

So she'd be so embarrassed and angry that the only thing left would be to turn it around to hurt him. She'd find the fire within…eventually.

But she could only do that if she made it through whatever this was.

The wedding planner bustled out of the room to "check on things." No doubt to try to track down Luciano. Serena let her. She wanted to be alone anyway. Blissfully alone in this little room.

Just her and a full-length mirror and a beautiful white gown, simple if not for the intricate lace details. Serena studied herself in said mirror. If she pretended to smile, a picture would show a beautiful, glowing bride, eager to start her new life.

But her face in the mirror right now showed the truth. The makeup could hide that she was pale. The white lace could give her an ethereal look. But her expression was all brittle ice because that was what she was made out of.

If she moved the wrong way, she would shatter. All because she'd fallen in love with the last man she should have.

That was on her. And she always took responsibility for her own mistakes.

So she stood, leaning into every last protective instinct. Detach, detach, detach. Don't let the pain through. It doesn't matter anyway.

You were always meant to be alone. It was stupid to be fooled into thinking otherwise.

It was something her mother would say if she was here. But, because of Luciano, Angelica was not here. She'd never apologized, and so she'd never been invited.

Tears pricked Serena's eyes at that thought, but she gripped her hands into fists and blinked them back. She would not cry. She'd rather *die*.

Before she could decide her next steps, the door creaked open. She looked at it in the mirror, still too fragile to move, then nearly fumbled right there at the sight of Luciano entering the room. But she didn't whirl. She didn't sob. She stood completely and utterly still and regarded his reflection in the mirror.

Their eyes met, held there.

He was *here*, and she knew better than to let her hopes soar. There was that grim set to his mouth, that haunted look in his eyes and the fact he wore now what he'd worn last night leaving her.

And carried a folder full of papers.

Serena inhaled carefully, bracing herself for all that was to come, then turned to face him. Every muscle in her was tense. But she kept her chin up and her eyes cool.

"The wedding planner is looking for you, I believe," she offered when he said nothing. Just stared at her. "And the wedding is due to start soon. Yet you are not dressed. You do not appear ready at all."

He blinked once, then twice, before looking down at the folder in his hand. Serena took this moment of him not looking at her to lower herself into a chair. Maybe if he couldn't see how gently she moved, he wouldn't see through her.

He took a step forward, held out the folder. "I have come to some new conclusions."

"I just bet," she murmured, and she absolutely refused to reach out and take those damn papers, whatever the hell they were.

"I do not need Ascione. You can have it."

He dropped the file of papers into her lap. She didn't want to touch it, so she hesitated, trying to work through his words. What he was saying.

What he wasn't saying.

I do not need Ascione might have been the words he said, but what she heard was *I do not need you*.

So she firmed her mouth, pulled the papers out of the folder. She took her time and made sure her voice would be clipped ice before she spoke.

"While it's good to come to this conclusion before we married under these false pretenses," she said, skimming the document and feeling a strange twist of emotions that she couldn't make sense of. Success. Failure. Love. Hate. And because there was so much inside of her, she treated him to ice when she looked up at him. "I do wish you'd done it before we'd planned everything. Before I'd gotten dressed."

His eyes roamed over her. "You look beautiful."

That just about broke whatever kept her temper firmly frozen, but she was too tired to start a fight. Too tired to do anything but survive.

She pressed a finger to her throbbing temple. "Why are you here, Luciano?"

"It is our wedding."

She snorted inelegantly, eyes still closed against the assault of all this. "I have the sneaking suspicion you weren't planning on attending."

For a moment, he said nothing. "I will not take the coward's way out," he said loftily. "I have given you Ascione outright. It would not do to have someone else deliver this news."

She laughed. It was a little bitter, maybe tinged with hysteria, but she laughed all the same. "What about the news that you don't plan to marry me?"

"You get Ascione."

She opened her eyes and looked up at him, staring for perhaps a full minute. He said it like it was a trade. She got his company. He got to not marry her. It shamed her and made her feel small, and she would have settled there. She would have accepted that.

Before.

Before he'd spent evenings with her watching the movies she liked. Before he'd gone with her to meet their—*her* future puppy. Before he had stood up for her and treated like she mattered. Not because of how smart she was, or what she could do or represent, but simply because of her.

Because of how he had recognized his own experiences in hers. And everything from that moment had felt real. The unfurling of something…wonderful and lasting.

The ice was melting, and she wanted—needed—to hold on to it, except she remembered what he'd said about his mother. About trying to save her.

That night had been the changing point. For both of them. She had realized someone might stand up for her, and she had thought he'd realized someone would allow him to.

But he hadn't. Whatever resolve he'd had faded, and that made her anger win. She stood, violently enough that the chair nearly toppled behind her. She stepped toward him, fury propelling her.

"Not take the coward's way out? You are nothing but a coward! But I do not for the life of me understand what you are afraid of." She shook the papers. "Success? Hope? Happiness? Commitment?" Despair wound through her, but it had nothing on fury. "A fake one at that."

"This is not fake, and you know it," he said starkly. "It has become…something else."

Oh, that should not make her heart soar, especially the despairing way he said it. And still… "A coward too afraid to say what is true. But I am not. You're afraid of love?"

"I am not *afraid*. I have chosen a course of action that will keep us both…" She watched him struggle for the word, when he never struggled for words.

"You have chosen to be an absolute idiot."

His mouth firmed. His eyes narrowed. There was anger there in his strained shoulders. "I have given you what you want. I have given you Ascione."

"I don't want—well, no, I still want Ascione." She could not lie about that. Holding the papers was like holding a golden goose. But it was still just a *thing*. She didn't only want a thing. "But I don't *only* want Ascione. I want *you* along with it. I want this—what we've built these past few weeks." She realized in this moment, that she had also been a coward. Because she had been waiting, putting off the inevitable, afraid to tell him what might drive him away.

And he'd driven himself away anyway, so why not drop the bomb he didn't want?

"Luciano, I love you. I think you might know that, but maybe you cannot fathom it. I love you. And I want to marry you. For you. With no worries or concerns about Ascione *or* Valli. I want there to be an us."

Luciano had prepared himself for many responses. Tears. Accusations. Violence, even. That is what he was used to when going into spaces he wasn't wanted.

He should have prepared himself for her ice, and maybe he had tried, but it had still hurt. Gotten under his skin in ways he'd convinced himself it wouldn't. But he'd been holding his own.

Until this.

He had not prepared himself for love. Even knowing she might have convinced herself she had some soft feelings for him, he had not assumed she would use it like…

"Why?" He had not meant to question this out loud. Hated the look of soft concern, too close to pity, that chased over her face.

"Luciano—"

"No." He slashed a hand through the air to get his point across. "No. I have made my choice, my decision. I have given you all that you wanted when you came into my club that night. From here on out, I will focus on my club, which is what *I* built. And you may focus on this." He gestured at the folder. "If your lawyers have qualms on the paperwork, my lawyer will be happy to discuss it with them. This…" He gestured between them. "This cannot be."

She did not have a quick retort to that. So he should leave. Take this silence for what it was and retreat.

His legs would not move. She was the most beautiful thing he'd ever seen. The dress was simple, but it made her look like an angel. She wore the ring he'd picked out for her and little pink diamonds on her ears that matched. He needed to leave because everything in him screamed to move forward, touch, grab.

Beg. For things he still did not fully understand.

Success? Hope? Happiness? Commitment?

She accused him of being afraid of those things. And love. Maybe he was, but it wasn't fear of having them that kept him rooted to the spot.

It was the fear of failing to hold on to these things that mattered. He could fail anyone and everyone. He had, to some extent. But he could not bear the thought of failing her.

"Cannot be," she finally murmured. "Why? What is it that would be so awful about getting married and loving one another? So awful that you would sign away your legacy, retreat to the caricature of yourself you created and pretend that you do not want all the things I know you do?"

It was everything he'd thought, and he did not understand. She couldn't… She couldn't possibly see him for who he was, no matter how right she was in this moment. "You do not know me. What I want."

"I do. Better than anyone," she replied in that clipped, calm way of hers. "Because I believe I am the only one you have ever actually been yourself around."

Yourself.

He shook his head—because he didn't know what being himself even was anymore, but he knew it couldn't be anything she wanted.

"Then you should have the good sense to take this deal and run, Serena. If you claim to know me, then you would know…" That no one ever loved him. That nothing he did or did not do could change how another person felt.

"I know that you are Luciano Ascione," she said, very firmly. "And I would never call you perfect, but I would certainly call you a good man. One whom I love."

Disgusted, he turned away from her. He wished he could turn away from himself. He did not know how this terrible swath of loathing that he had kept at bay for so many years had somehow grown instead of dying away. "You are the only one."

"Then so be it. I will gladly be the only one." There was fire in her now, blazing from within. "Do you think that matters to me?" she demanded, grabbing his arm and jerking him back to face her. "Me of all people? What anyone else thinks? When I know you? No one else matters."

"How could you know me, Serena?" he demanded, finding his own anger in this whole mess that she would not let him handle appropriately. "I am not certain, after all this, that I know myself."

"Then let me save you this time, Luciano," she said, softer this time. "Let me stand between you and the things others have said about you. You are clever and kind. You are an arrogant bastard when you want to be, but it is not mean. And I think, perhaps, what you are most afraid of is not your own shortcomings so much as the fact you do not know what to do with this."

"With what?"

"You love me, Luciano. This scares you, but it doesn't make you less."

There was an anvil on his chest. Something lodged in his throat. Love. *Love*. This useless emotion that was never, ever reciprocated.

Except she'd already said she loved him. How she could, he did not know, but Serena did not lie. She did not exaggerate. And still…

"Loving me doesn't scare you?" he demanded in a rasp.

"Of course it does," she said, in that same confident and unbothered way she confessed any of her odd little idiosyncrasies. "But being scared is no reason to run away in business, so why should it be in life?"

"You cannot run life like a business." He thought he sounded very sure and worldly then, but she only rolled her eyes. There in her *wedding dress*. Arguing with him about love instead of taking this deal and running.

Like she should.

Like he'd expected her to.

Like he'd *needed* her to in order to survive this rising tide of hope that he knew would end in pain.

Pain.

"I do not see why not," she replied haughtily. "It's all the same. Keep something alive and thriving for as long as you can. Show up every day, work through problems without giving up. It *is* the same. Except for one thing. One matters, Luciano. I…" She inhaled deeply, took a moment, and her eyes were shining now. Which always undid him. It was unfair. To be undone by this woman.

"I had my grandfather when he was alive," she said, her voice quiet now. "And he was also not perfect, but I know he cared for me in his way. And that has meant more than all the successes I ever found at Valli. Because love and care are more important than profits and clients. I have no one now. No one to love and care for—except my animals. And you."

She said it softly, but it landed like a vise around his lungs.

"I could run a Valli-Ascione merger without you. It would be hard, meticulous work. I could do it. I *will* do it if you insist on ruining everything, but you will not walk out of this room under the very wrong conclusion that you have saved us from anything. If you walk, you ruin it. What could be. The future we've both been a little too afraid to admit is possible, but I won't be afraid any longer. What about you?"

She did not understand. Could not. Except every word she said made it feel like she did. But how could he sentence them to this…this…certain disappointment? "Serena."

"You have two choices. You may stay. Get dressed for the wedding and marry me, knowing that we have work ahead of us. A business merger and a life merger. That includes a wide variety of animals, now and in the future. That includes love and difficulties and joy. And children. I think I would like to have children with you."

Children. Just the idea of it sent opposing feelings through him. An icy, paralyzing fear. And a warmth of hope and joy that threatened to melt it.

Children with her brains, her eyes. Children. Theirs. A family. One that would not look like theirs had growing up.

It was impossible. She was saying it was possible, but how could it be? How could it be with him?

"Or you may walk out that door," she continued, when he stood there paralyzed by her words. "But you will not walk back in it." She said this fiercely, and he could see she meant it. She needed to mean it. "Ascione will be gone from you forever." She clutched the papers. "And so will I be. I suggest you make that decision wisely."

Gone forever. Even though that's what he'd planned, the idea of it—with her standing there in white, looking like a beautiful angel, looking like everything that had filled his life with warmth and worth for the past few weeks—cleaved through him like a blade.

She represented everything that had changed him. Brought him back to life after lying dormant under that caricature. Or perhaps she'd simply taken a moment to see behind the mask, because she held up one of her own.

And because it was her, and because she was annoyingly always so right, he realized that it was more than what she'd done for *him*. He wasn't saving her from *him*, because… This was not one-sided. It was not parent to child.

It was partners.

He had melted her ice. He had stood up for her when she had been fighting alone for so long.

Was that why she loved him? How she could? He had… offered the same thing to her as she had to him. Just like under all their surface differences, they were so much the same.

He supposed it made as much sense as anything. And maybe it was selfish. Maybe that horrible disappointment was waiting for both of them. The fear of it nearly had him walking out.

But he was more afraid of walking out that door and being refused reentry. Because he believed her. She would not give him a second chance. He would not deserve one.

So maybe…like she said, they could show up every day and work on it. If there was anyone in this world he trusted to do that, it was Serena.

Serena. The woman he loved.

"It sounds like blackmail, Serena," he managed to say, though his throat was still tight. "Is that any way to start a life?"

She didn't smile like he wanted her to, but there was

something in her eyes. Something warm. "All in all? It sounds very on brand for any Valli-Ascione interaction."

He could not help himself. He laughed. He did not know how he could when it felt as if all his safe foundations were crumbling, except that she made everything…better. Right. Just by being her. And if she could be brave, if she could love him, did he not owe it to her to do the same?

She moved forward, reached out and gripped his arms. She even gave him a little shake, her expression earnest. "Stay. Love me," she said, and it was a demand, but he was not one to be demanded into doing anything.

Unless he already did. "I do," he replied, as seriously as the vows he would soon say. "Love you."

"I know. I'd just take the business if you didn't," she replied haughtily, making him smile.

He pushed a strand of hair behind her ear, studied her beautiful face. "I will make mistakes."

"Horrible ones," she agreed.

"And you will ice me out."

"Most assuredly."

"And we will…show up every day and try in spite of ourselves."

"Every day," she agreed, reaching up to cup his face.

His hands shook as he reached out, as he placed them on her hips, held on to her. His match. His mate. His everything. "Marry me, then, Serena. For real. For love."

Her eyes were full, but she did not cry. "For us," she agreed, and then put her mouth to his.

EPILOGUE

THEY MARRIED IN a splashy society wedding that was the talk of the town, but they said their true vows before—in that little room. When they thought of their wedding, they thought of that.

Because they were happy to give the public that which would suit Valli-Ascione, but it was not the *truth* of them.

Together, they slowly rebuilt their father's destroyed legacies. Until, as the years past, they built their own legacy. Not in any boardrooms or shipping containers, but in their home. The castle on the hill. Full to the brim of animals, and then a handful of children.

And through both, they learned how to love, and how to show it. How to believe and hope, even in spite of the challenges and griefs of life.

They encouraged their children to be their truest selves, and accepted each of them exactly as they were, no matter what challenges arose. They protected and stood up for each other. And when they fought—ice and fire—they always made up on the foundation of love they spent their entire lives building. Showing up, day after day.

It was the *new* Valli-Ascione legacy, rising from the ashes of the old.

Made with love. The kind that lasted lifetimes.

* * * * *